SPALDING®

I can do
GYMNASTICS

E DUE

Essential Skills for Intermediate Gymnasts

USA Gymnastics

MASTERS PRESS

A Division of Howard W. Sams & Co.

S

Published by Masters Press (A Division of Howard W. Sams)
2647 Waterfront Pkwy E. Dr., Suite 300, Indianapolis, IN 46214

Library of Congress Cataloging-in-Publication Data

I can do gymnastics: essential skills for intermediate gymnasts/
USA Gymnastics.
        p. cm. -- (Spalding sports library)
ISBN 0-940279-54-1: $12.95
1. Gymnastics. I. U.S.A. Gymnastics.
II. Series.
GV461.I2 1992   92-43281
796.44—dc20   CIP

Credits:
Illustrations by Steve Whitlock.
Photos by Dave Calisch of Calisch Photography.
Chapter one, "Safety Landing Skills" adapted from *Gymnastics: A Guide for
Parents and Athletes* by Rik Feeney, published 1992 by Masters Press. Illus-
trations in chapter one by Lynn Wilton.
Cover design by Christy Pierce.

This copy of *I CAN DO GYMNASTICS*
Essential Skills for Intermediate Gymnasts
belongs to:

Name _____

Street Address _____

City, State, Zip _____

Telephone Number   (   )_____

Date of Birth _____

Age _____ Grade in School _____

My Coaches are _____

_____

_____

My Club is _____

Table of Contents

Acknowledgments

Thank you to the many contributing authors:

Patty Hacker, South Dakota State University, Brookings, SD

Eric Malmerg, State University College, Cortland, NY

Jim Nance, University of Kentucky, Lexington, KY

Alan Tilove, National School Assemblies, Valencia, CA

Susan True, National Federation of State High School Associations,
Kansas City, MO

Terry Exner, GymMarin, San Rafael, CA

Steve Whitlock, Director of Educational Services and Safety,
USA Gymnastics, Indianapolis, IN

Dave Moskovitz, Coaching Development Coordiator,
USA Gymnastics, Indianapolis, IN

Preface

In Europe, gymnastics is considered the basis for all physical education! Unfortunately, in the United States, gymnastics has come to be identified by both educators and the general public by what they see on television — the Olympic events of competitive Artistic Gymnastics.

The authors of the *I Can Do Gymnastics* series are physical educators with a love and background in gymnastics who understand and appreciate the movement benefits of incorporating a broader definition of gymnastics in the school curriculum.

The goal of *I Can Do Gymnastics* is to present a series of gymnastics activities from a movement education point-of-view. Sub-goals include selection of skills and sequences that follow a movement education philosophy, that are transferable to other sports and lifetime activity interests, and that increase the health benefits of U.S. children. Further considerations include equipment cost and availability, safety, facilities, teacher background and experience, spotting needs, and an enjoyable program.

The *I Can Do Gymnastics* program was originally designed with the elementary school teacher in mind. However, early experience with the program has indicated that it has even broader implications and applications. Gymnastics clubs are beginning to utilize the program with their instructional/recreational classes because the concepts develop good gymnastics. Several universities and colleges have also started to incorporate *I Can Do Gymnastics* into their offerings as elective physical education classes and/or as movement and majors classes.

USA Gymnastics hopes that the students and educators will find this program to be popular and beneficial.

How to Use this Program

I Can Do Gymnastics: Essential Skills for Intermediate Gymnasts is an extension of the USA Gymnastics' "Sequential Gymnastics II" program. The purpose of these activities is to expand the movement vocabulary of children through sequential gymnastics activities presented in a safe and fun environment.

The content of this book follows developmentally the skills and movement sequences introduced in *I Can Do Gymnastics: Essential Skills for Beginning Gymnasts.* Students should demonstrate mastery and confidence in performing the beginning skills before attempting the intermediate or advanced skills and sequences.

Safety is the most important aspect of any gymnastics program. Safety considerations are built into the skill sequences included in this book. The sequences progress skill by skill, each building on the last and each sequence selected because it requires minimal or no spotting (assistance). Skills are to be learned as listed in progressive order, beginning with Skill One, Level of Difficulty A in each category of movement.

The activities in each movement category, for example the "Upright Balance Skills" in chapter two, are *internalized* by the gymnast before progressing to the next skill. *Internalizing* a skill means that the gymnast can perform the skill easily and without much concerted effort. This ensures that the gymnast is always ready to move to the next skill and has confidence in his or her own ability to perform.

3

The second part of this book is an "Advanced Supplement." This section provides the instructor with suggestions for skill development on other common gymnastics apparatus such as the uneven bars, parallel bars, rings, pommel horse, as well as more advanced tumbling skills.

The skills in the advanced supplement are presented sequentially from beginning to the more advanced skills. Students should practice each skill until mastery before progressing to the next skill or sequence.

I Can Do Gymnastics is intended to be used as a guideline for parents and gymnasts so that they might learn more about gymnastics while monitoring their own progress in the sport. The program is effective only when used in the proper setting and by people with the appropriate training to teach and train young gymnasts.

Steve Whitlock
Director of Educational Services and Safety
U.S.A. Gymnastics

For the Gymnast

I Can Do Gymnastics: Essential Skills for Intermediate Gymnasts is a step by step way for you to learn new gymnastics skills and sequences. You should have completed all of the skills in *I Can Do Gymnastics: Essential Skills for Beginning Gymnasts* prior to learning the skills presented in this book.

Each chapter starts with some of the easier skills presented in the first *I Can Do* book. Next, more difficult skills are introduced, and finally, selected skills are combined into movement sequences. Each skill and sequence builds on those before it, so be sure that you can do a skill well by yourself before you move on to the next one.

Always start with "A" level skills and skill "1" when you begin a section. Just because you think you know how to do a skill already doesn't mean you understand how to do it the safest and the best way. If you progress from one skill to the next and get checked on each skill by your coach as you go through each level, you will be sure to be learning the skills the right way. This results in less problems later on.

This book is really designed to compliment the gymnastics program at your club or school. Most require special equipment and assistance that only a professional coach and club will have. You will need help on a lot of these skills when you start doing them because you could get hurt trying them without proper help from a professional gymnastics coach. Your coach will know the best way to "spot" you on a skill. Gyms also usually have all the right kinds of equipment in your size and with the right kind of mats and other safety equipment in case you fall.

There are some skills that you can practice at home. As a gymnast you need to work on becoming stronger and improving your coordination and flexibility. Your coach can recommend some activities that you can safely perform at home that will help your gymnastics progress.

Remember: the most important thing in gymnastics is your safety. If you are ever scared or don't think you can do a trick, tell your coach. Your coach will make sure that everything will be done to make you feel safe and prepared to complete every skill.

1
Equipment

The skills listed in *I Can Do Gymnastics* were selected because, for the most part, they can be performed on a wide range of reasonably priced equipment that can be found in many gym clubs and schools. Besides the "regulation" gymnastics equipment that is required in competitive gymnastics programs, most of the skills can be performed on less expensive "junior" equipment or even using combinations of "skill builder" mat shapes that are often utilized in preschool movement education programs. For example, the vaulting skills may be performed on a standard gymnastics vaulting horse, or if it is not available, the teacher can utilize stacked folding mats or a trapezoid as alternatives.

It is important that a gymnast be familiar with the equipment used while participating in gymnastics. Skills must always be practiced in a safe and secure environment. Using proper equipment that is set correctly is one of the best ways to ensure a safe performance.

Mats

When selecting mats, it is important to ensure that the mats that you are using are appropriate for the activities and placed to provide the utmost safety. A list of the descriptions of the most commonly used mats follow.

Panel (folding) mats These come in assorted sizes and colors. The most common sizes for folding panel mats are five by ten feet, or six by twelve feet. These mats are used as resilient tumbling or exercise surfaces, under gymnastics apparatus to provide a zone of safety if a participant falls from the equipment, or folded for special situations. The best mats have special velcro fasteners at each end so that the mats can be linked to prevent gaps, cracks, or slippage.

Spring-type floor These are specially designed mat systems used in competitive gymnastics that provide an excellent rebounding surface. They are commonly found in gym clubs or schools with competitive gymnastics programs.

Landing mats Common sizes are five by ten feet by four to six inches. They are constructed with a firm layer of foam over a softer layer in order to provide an absorbent landing surface for performing landings from dismounts or to provide extra protection from falls from the apparatus. These mats are used under apparatus to protect against falls or in the "landing" areas where dismounts are performed.

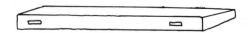

Skill cushions These mats often look like landing mats, but are designed with a soft foam core which make them ideal for "body landings" as opposed to foot landings. The standard five by ten feet and six by twelve dimensions are common. The height of the mats vary from eight to thirty-two inches. These mats are often stacked to various heights to provide safety or to be utilized for special learning situations when teaching new skills.

　　　　　　　I CAN DO GYMNASTICS

Skill Builder Mats (Shapes)

These are becoming very popular because of their versatility, price, mobility, and safety features. They are usually constructed of a firm (but not hard) foam core covered with a rugged but colorful vinyl material. The most popular shapes are as follows.

Wedge This is essentially an incline plane. It is a wonderful mat to utilize when teaching many new skills.

Trapezoid This shape can be used as an alternative for many vaulting situations, as "obstacles," and even as platforms for the teacher to stand on when spotting skills. Most are designed to be broken-down into various useful heights. A typical size is five by six feet by twenty inches.

Blocks These mats come in all sizes, from two by two by one foot to four by eight by two feet. Their use is limited only by the imagination of the instructor.

Vaulting Board

These are known by many names: spring board, vaulting board, mounting board, beat board, and "Reuther" board. Their primary use is as a device to mount the apparatus or gain height when learning tumbling and vaulting skills. The "regulation" size is three by four feet by ten inches, but many suppliers offer "junior" sizes for lighter weight participants.

Vaulting Horse(s)

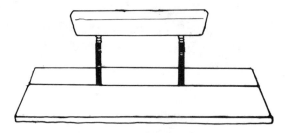

The apparatus used for vaulting is called a horse. Adjustable in height, most advanced performers use the vault at 47.25 inches (about four feet). However, beginning vaulting skills may not even be practiced with a horse. Instead, beginners may use stacked panel mats or a trapezoid.

Once gymnasts have learned the basic skills, men and women may begin to work on the different equipment associated with competitive gymnastics. All beginners use the horse sideways. In competitive gymnastics, women continue to use the **Side Horse Vault**, but in men's competitive gymnastics the horse is positioned lengthwise and is called **Long Horse Vaulting**.

Horizontal or Single Bar

Your first bar skills will be performed on a low horizontal bar that adjusts from three to five feet in height. How high the bar is set will depend on your size (not you ability) and the skills being performed. The bar itself, also called the "rail," may be made from wood, steel, or a special wood/fiberglass combination. In competitive gymnastics, the women utilize the **Uneven Parallel Bars**, while the men compete on both the **Parallel Bars** and the **High Horizontal Bar**.

I CAN DO GYMNASTICS

Balance Beam

The balance beam is made of a long narrow piece of wood or metal that is usually covered with a thin piece of foam and a suede leather or synthetic fabric. The standard beam measures four inches wide and sixteen feet long and stands on a steel base that can adjust up to four and a quarter feet high. Most suppliers provide inexpensive "low" beams or "junior" beams that vary in height from six to eight inches to thirty-two inches in height. Most of the skills in *I Can Do Gymnastics* are designed to be performed on low to intermediate height beams. It is strongly suggested that any skills to be performed on a beam first be mastered on the floor, then on a line on the floor, and finally on progressively higher beams.

The beam is an excellent apparatus for beginners (girls and boys) to develop balancing skills. Once the basics are mastered, the girls will continue to work toward the achievement of higher level skills and combinations since the beam is one of the competitive events for Women's Artistic Gymnastics. The boys, however, will devote less and less attention to this apparatus since it is not one of the Men's Artistic Events in competitive gymnastics.

ADVANCED SUPPLEMENT APPARATUS

One of the reasons for the development of the Advanced Supplement to *I Can Do Gymnastics* was the interest by many teachers to have suggestions for using other gymnastics equipment that they might have available. Most of this apparatus is designed primarily for use in competitive gymnastics programs. Therefore, you will note that the illustrations emphasize use by boys on the rings, pommel horse, and parallel bars, and the uneven bars emphasize use by girls. However, the early progressions in *I Can Do Gymnastics* present **basic** gymnastics movement that is challenging, appropriate, and fun for both genders. Boys and girls are encouraged to utilize the beginning skills on all the apparatus presented in the Advanced Supplement.

Uneven Parallel Bars.

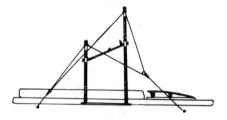

This apparatus will be a challenge to all who have accomplished the basics on the single bar. Because of the nature and height of the apparatus, it is recommended that standard equipment be used. Suppliers do provide "junior" equipment, but be careful to follow the recommended guidelines regarding participant size and weight.

Parallel Bars

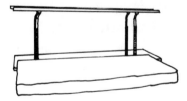

While this apparatus is considered a "men's" event, the basic skills can be performed by both boys and girls. The event encourages the development of upper body strength, support positions, and basic swing technique. It is a good general movement development apparatus since there are large numbers of basic skills that are fun to do and require minimal support strength to accomplish.

If you don't have a set of parallel bars, many of the skills can be learned and performed with two balance beams or two stacks of mats set side-by-side. A few suppliers even manufacture special skill builder mats designed to be used as alternatives to regulation or "junior" parallel bars.

Rings

This apparatus is suspended from the ceiling or from a special free standing support stand. The regulation height of the rings is approximately eight feet above the floor. However, **it is very important that beginners only use rings that can be adjusted to the lower heights suggested in the Advanced Supplement**.

Even though the rings are considered a men's competitive apparatus, girls will both enjoy and benefit from learning the basic skills.

Pommel Horse

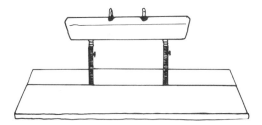

This men's competitive apparatus is difficult to master since it requires considerable upper-body strength and is somewhat unique in the physical and technical requirements for mastery of more than the basic skills.

However, in women's competitive gymnastics, we are now seeing performers who are transferring pommel horse-type moves with great success and originality onto the balance beam and even floor exercises.

2

Safety Landing Skills

Falling and landing skills are perhaps the most important skills to learn in gymnastics. Practice these basic drills until you master the basic safety landing positions. You can then use the safety skills when you are performing other sports. You will be less likely to get hurt when playing other sports with your friends, or on the playground if you know how to fall correctly.

When first learning the following safety drills, make sure you are practicing them under the supervision of your coach. Your coach will make sure that you are learning how to land and fall correctly.

SAFETY LANDING DRILLS

The basic safety landing drills are:

1) **Basic Safety Landing Position (or SLP)**: The basic position to land from a skill is to stand mostly upright with the arms up next to the ears (to help protect the neck and head), the knees flexed to a 45° angle, the stomach sucked in, weight on the full foot, but not flat-footed or on the toes, and the lower back slightly rounded.

It is important to remember that the back is always rounded and the knees flexed upon landing, otherwise the force of the landing can severely jar your lower back, possibly causing injury.

Note: When practicing these Safety Landing Drills, always begin from a low surface such as a folded up mat and progressively work up to a higher surface such as a balance beam. Don't jump off anything that is higher than your waist until you are completely comfortable with landing technique.

No matter which basic landing drill you are practicing, always remember that you should try to land on your feet first!

Basic SLP

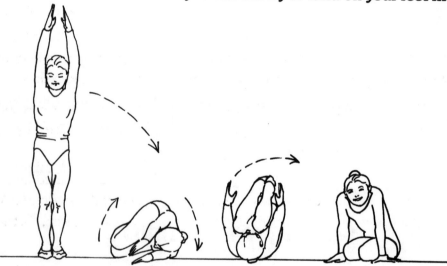

SLP with a Side Roll

2) **SLP with a Side Roll**: This safety landing is used when you over-rotate when landing. To practice: Lay on the mat on your back and bring both knees up to your chest. Roll completely over in a sideways direction. Next: Practice landing in SLP then going into a sideways roll. Practice rolling to both sides.

Note: When you start practicing this skill, you may want to grab your knees to do the side roll. Remember that you should keep your arms up to protect your head and practice the skill that way.

3) **Backward SLP**: This is the same as the basic SLP except that you are landing with rotation in a backward direction.

Note: Be sure that when you practice jumping backwards you keep your head

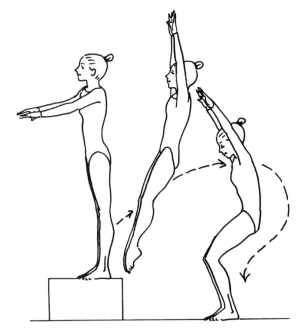

Backward SLP

up. Many gymnasts have a tendency to look down which could cause them to strike their head on the equipment they are jumping from. Remember to always work up from lower to higher platforms in practicing these skills.

4) **Backward SLP with Tuck and Roll**: Lay on the floor with knees and hips flexed, lower back rounded, and arms up above the head. Practice rocking back and forth in this position.

Next, jump off a raised surface landing in Backward SLP, and continue through to the floor rocking backwards (without going over) then rolling back up to a stand. Do not roll over all the way as it is very easy to compress the neck in this position.

Try to remember to always protect the head, neck, and back first when you fall.

Hand Position: When over-rotating a landing the hands may be placed on the ground to help guide the body into the roll which will break the force of the fall. The hands should not be used to catch the entire body weight during a fall. Practice closing fists when you fall from the apparatus so that you will not try to roll or break a fall with a partially open hand. Remember to keep your fingers facing forward so that your elbows will flex.

Backward SLP with Tuck and Roll

Falling Backward: Never place the arms behind the body with the elbows locked. This invites serious injury to the wrist and elbow and possible dislocation of the shoulder. If the hands are placed on the floor during a backwards rotating fall, the hands should be placed at the sides of the body with the fingers pointing towards the toes so that the elbows can flex as the body rolls backward.

Horizontal or Uneven Bars: Practice each of the drills from a small swing on the bars. Falling from a swing can be a much different experience than falling from other pieces of apparatus. A gymnast may fall off going in a forward direction while their body rotates backward or vice-versa on the bars. When dismounting, you should always release the bar at the peak of your swing, not while you are still rising in the swing.

Note: Initially all these skills should be practiced under the strict supervision of a qualified gymnastics coach and competent spotter.

3

The Warm-Up

Warming-up is an important preparation for any sport activity. The purpose of the warm-up is to raise the body core temperature and generally prepare the body for more strenuous activity. It is believed that warm-up not only assists the athlete in good performance but decreases the likelihood of injury. It is a good idea to divide warm-up time between three basic activities: aerobics, stretching, and preparation for the next activity.

AEROBICS

The aerobic part of the warm-up can last anywhere from three to twenty minutes. The individual performs light continuous activities during this period. Typical exercises include jogging, running, skipping, hopping, and jumping jacks. The aerobic part of the warm-up can include games, relays, and even dances or other rhythmic activities to music — as long as the activities are easy and continuous and get the participants "breathing heavy," almost any activity is permissible.

In group situations, the teacher may decide to use a very structured approach and have all of the students perform the same activities at the same time, or a less structured approach and allow the individuals more freedom.

STRETCHING

The stretching portion of the warm-up should follow the aerobic portion. The purpose of the stretching session is merely to establish range of motion of all joints, **not** to increase or improve range of motion. The more intense stretching is usually done at the end of a training period when the muscles are fatigued.

Therefore, warm-up stretches should be light. A good rule of thumb is to begin with the extremities and then work towards the center of the body. For example, wrist rotations precede shoulder stretches, which precede trunk stretches.

When stretching a muscle, **GO SLOW**! Bouncing, vigorous swinging, or other dynamic stretching activities can be dangerous and result in muscle strains or sprains. The best idea is to slowly stretch the muscle to the individual's personal limit and then hold this position for six to ten counts. (Repeat each stretch three times.) Some common stretches for warm-up are illustrated below.

Wrist and Ankle Stretches

- Slowly rotate the wrists outward, then outward for a minimum of five rotations. Repeat this exercise with the ankles.
- Sitting or standing, place the palms together, interlock the fingers, and rotate the wrists, making large circles around the hands.
- Dance stretches: Pliés and relevés in all the positions of the feet.

Side and Shoulder Stretches

- Stand with one arm extended straight up. Tilt the body to the opposite side reaching the hand up and across. (Repeat on the other side.)

- Extend one arm across the chest, grasp the raised elbow with the opposite hand, and pull the elbow backward. (Repeat on the other side.)
- Dance Stretches: Port de bras.

Forward and Rear Shoulder Stretches

- Using a low bar or other suitable substitute, grasp the bar with the hands about shoulder width apart. Flex forward at the waist, allowing the shoulders to rotate inward and the chest to drop below the bar.

- Using a low bar or substitute, stand facing away from the bar. Grasp the bar with the hands slightly beyond shoulder width and thumbs facing out. Slowly push the knees and hips out away from the bar. Allow the shoulders and the back to drop below the bar.
- Dance Stretches: Port de bras.

Half Split Stretch

- In a forward lunge, touch the back knee to the mat keeping the head and shoulders upright. Then, extend the forward leg in order to stretch the hamstring while flexing the chest forward. (Repeat on the other side.)

- For a variation, flex the back leg to 90° in order to stretch the quadriceps muscle. This is more easily done if you use one hand to assist by pulling on the foot of the back leg. (Repeat on the other side.)

- Dance Stretches: Tendus, battements, and grand pliés.

Modified Hurdle and Hip Stretch

- Sitting on the mat in a straddle (approximately 90°), bend one leg inward, positioning the heel against the opposite thigh. Flex at the waist forward over the extended leg. (Repeat on the other side.)

- Sit in a 135° straddle and slowly stretch forward and to each side.

Neck Stretches

- Chin to chest: Slowly lower the head forward, press the chin toward the chest, then raise the head.

- Ear to shoulder: Slowly lower the head to the side, press the ear toward the shoulder and raise the head.

- Dance Stretches: Port de bras

PREPARATION FOR THE NEXT ACTIVITY

The warm-up is not an end in itself, but it leads into the next activity. Therefore, as the aerobic and stretching portions of the warm-up conclude, the student will continue with selected exercises and movements from their next activity. For example, if the next activity is tumbling, the student might perform basic rolls, balances, and body positions. This leads logically into review or rehearsal (practice) of previously learned skills.

If the student is proceeding on to the single bar, preparations might include hangs and basic swings prior to progressing to more difficult or new skills.

COOL-DOWN

At the conclusion of the training period or lesson, it is advisable to allow the body to "cool-down." Very mild activities are used while the body cools and the pulse and breathing rates return to normal. Common activities for the cool-down include some easy games, light jogging, or just walking.

4

Tumbling Skills and Sequences

UPRIGHT BALANCE SKILLS

Level of Difficulty: A

1 **Balance on One Foot (left/right)** Stand on the extended support leg. Hold two or three counts with free leg in optional position.

What to Practice:
- Focus the eyes on a single point while balancing - don't look around!
- Support leg should be extended.
- Whole body should remain completely still.

2 **Relevé Stands** Balance on half toe for two or three counts on one or both feet in a stand position. (Arms optional.)

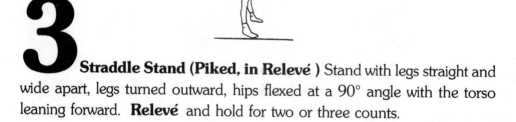

3 **Straddle Stand (Piked, in Relevé)** Stand with legs straight and wide apart, legs turned outward, hips flexed at a 90° angle with the torso leaning forward. **Relevé** and hold for two or three counts.

UPRIGHT BALANCE SKILLS

Level of Difficulty: B

4 **Lunge to Arabesque, Rise to Relevé** From a lunge position, lift the rear leg back and up while extending the support leg to show a low arabesque position. While in arabesque, relevé and hold for two or three counts.

5 **Promenade** While maintaining a low arabesque, sequentially complete a full turn outward in quarters or in eighths. (Be sure to show stable arabesque balance after each partial turn.)

6 **Sissone to Scale (two seconds)** From a stand, Plié and jump forward extending the legs to a diagonal split position with the rear leg high and the front leg low. Land on the forward leg in demi-plié passing through low arabesque. Step forward into a front scale and hold for two or three counts.

UPRIGHT BALANCE SKILLS

Level of Difficulty: C

7 **Chassé Backward, Chassé to the Side, Fouetté (hold low arabesque)**

> *What to practice:*
> - Rhythmic movements.
> - Stable arm positions.
> - Balance in final arabesque.

8 **Side Scale into Side Cartwheel** Hold side scale for two or three counts, lift extended leg higher and reach hands to the side to the floor and execute a cartwheel to a stand. Practice in both directions.

9 **Side Scale, Cartwheel, Side Scale** Repeat skill number eight, but finish cartwheel in a side scale position on the opposite leg.

BALANCING STRENGTH SKILLS

Level of Difficulty: A

1 **Tuck Balance on Hands** From a kneeling position sitting on the heels, hands placed beside the hips on the mat, press against the floor with the hands to hold the body off the mat. Maintain body in tuck position. (May also be practiced from a tucked kneeling position.)

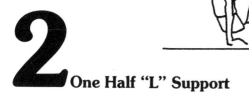

2 **One Half "L" Support**

3 **"L" Support** From a pike-sit position with the hands placed on the mat slightly in front of the hips, press against the floor with the hands to hold the body off the mat. Maintain pike ("L") position with legs parallel to the floor.

BALANCING STRENGTH SKILLS

Level of Difficulty: B

4 "L" Support in Straddle (inside or out) From a straddle pike-sit position with hands placed on the mat either between the legs or outside the hips, press against the floor with the hands to hold the body off the mat. Maintain straddle pike position with legs parallel to the floor.

5 "L" Support to Squat to Stand From a pike-sit, press to an "L" support. Flex the knees and rotate the body backward to place feet on the floor between the hands. Extend the body to stand.

6 Tuck Balance to Hip Press From a tuck balance position, press the hips back and up to head height or above. Return to tuck balance position.

BALANCING STRENGTH SKILLS

Level of Difficulty: C

7 **Tuck Balance, With a Press to Straddle Stand** From a tuck balance position, press the hips to head height or above while straightening and straddling legs to arrive in straddle stand.

> *What to practice:*
> * Straight arm support.
> * Keep the hip raise a continuous motion.
> * Feet remain off the floor during the press.

8 **Kneeling Half Pike Presses** From a kneeling position sitting on the heels, place hands on the mat just outside the knees. Slowly press hips up while straightening legs until the toes barely touch the floor. Hold this position for two or three counts.

9 **Squat Jump (Press) to Handstand against a Wall** From a squat stand facing the wall, place the hands on the mat while extending the legs to jump (press) instead into a handstand position with the back against the wall.

UPRIGHT AGILITY SKILLS

Level of Difficulty: A

1

Stride Leap From two or three steps, push off one foot to rise in the air. Land on the opposite (forward) foot with the knee slightly flexed.

2

Fouetté Step forward, swing the rear leg forward and upward toward the horizontal. Turn 180° to land on the foot of the push-off leg.

> *What to practice:*
>
> - Bend the takeoff leg to jump (demi-plié).
> - Maintain body alignment.
> - Land in plié

3

Tourjeté Jump from one foot to the other foot while performing a 180° turn switching legs in the air. Land in an arabesque on the foot of the first leg lifted in the air.

UPRIGHT AGILITY SKILLS

Level of Difficulty: B

4 **Cabriole** Takeoff from one foot, extending the other leg and foot forward in the air, torso upright. Bring rear leg up and forward, touching calves of both legs in the air. Land on both feet, knees slightly flexed, keeping torso upright. This step may also be performed to the side and/or after several running steps.

5 **Skip Sequence** A series of step hops, as follows: step left, hop on left foot placing right foot at left ankle; step right, hop on right foot placing left foot at right knee; step left, hop on left foot extending right leg up and forward; step right, hop on right foot and extend left leg up and to the rear.

6 **Chassé-Fouetté** Extend one foot forward, push off the floor with the same foot. Close the back foot behind the front foot in the air, then land on the back foot (gallop with height). Immediately step forward onto the front foot, swing rear leg forward and up toward horizontal. Turn 180° in the air to land on foot of the push-off leg (fouetté).

UPRIGHT AGILITY SKILLS

Level of Difficulty: C

chassé, hitchkick

7 **Sissone-Chassé-Hitchkick** Step forward, jump off both feet extending the legs to a diagonal split position (rear leg high, front leg low) and land in low arabesque. Swing the rear leg forward, step forward on that leg and push off the floor to perform a chassé. Land on the rear foot, step forward onto the front foot, swing the rear leg forward and up to jump from one foot to the other while switching legs in the air in front of the body (hitchkick). Land on one foot.

8 **Run-Assemblé-Tuck Jump-Step Out** Take several running steps forward, jump from one foot swinging the free leg forward. Bring the feet together in the air and land on the mat in demi-plié (assemblé). Immediately, push off from two feet to perform a tuck jump (knees forward and up). Land on two feet, step forward, and push off the mat to perform a forward chassé.

9 **Back Hitchkick-Chassé-Side Slide-Cartwheel** Push off from one foot to the other, switching legs in the air behind the body (back hitchkick). Land on the mat on one foot. Immediately swing the free leg forward, step forward, and push off the mat into the air to perform forward chassé. Land on one foot, and turn 90° to the right and perform one slide step left. Cartwheel left and land in an upright standing position.

FORWARD ROLLING SKILLS WITH A WEDGE OR STACKED MATS

Level of Difficulty: A

1 **Slide Down from Stacked Mats** From a prone position on the stack, with the head and shoulders extended beyond the stack, place hands on the floor mat and slide the body forward over the edge of the stack to execute a forward roll on the upper back to a stand.

2 **Jump to a Forward Roll to Lying Position on Stacked Mats** Stand on the floor mat facing the stack with the hands placed on the top of the stack. Jump from the floor, lifting the hips to execute a forward roll to finish lying on the stack in a supine position.

3 **Jump to a Forward Roll to Sit on Stacked Mats** Stand on the floor mat facing the stack with hands placed on the top of the stack. Jump from the floor, lifting the hips to execute a forward roll. Finish in a sit position on mats.

FORWARD ROLLING SKILLS WITH A WEDGE OR STACKED MATS

Level of Difficulty: B

4 **Jump to Forward Straddle Roll to Sit on Stacked Mats** Stand on the floor mat facing the stack with the hands placed on the mats. Jump from the floor, lifting the hips to execute a forward straddle roll to finish in a straddle sit position.

5 **Jump to Headstand Position and Roll-Out** Jump to headstand position on stacked mats. Show handstand position and then push with the hands to elevate the body to execute a forward roll to a stand.

What to practice:
- Maintain support on the hands throughout headstand.
- Continue forward body motion.
- Keep body weight off the head on the forward roll.

6 **Jump to a Headstand, Roll, and Step-out** Jump to headstand position on stacked mats. Execute a forward roll with step-out.

I CAN DO GYMNASTICS

FORWARD ROLLING SKILLS WITH A WEDGE OR STACKED MATS

Level of Difficulty: C

7 **Running Steps to Jump, Forward Roll** From two or three running steps, bring the feet together and jump into forward roll with hands for support on the stacked mats. Finish position optional.

8 **Running Steps to Jump, Pike Forward Roll** From two or three running steps, bring the feet together and jump into a pike forward roll with hands on stacked mats for support. Finish position optional.

What to practice:
- Initiate jump with flexed legs.
- Maintain support on the hands while initiating a roll.
- Keep entire movement under control.

9 **Running Steps to Jump, Pike Forward Roll on an Elevated Mat** From two or three running steps, bring the feet together and jump into a pike forward roll with hands on elevated end of stacked mats for support. Finish position is optional. (Skill may be performed on stacked mats or on a wedge.)

FORWARD ROLLING OVER SKILLS

Level of Difficulty: A

1 **Straddle Forward Roll** Stand with feet together and reach out approximately one half of your body length with hands on the mat. When your hands contact the floor, push off the legs and simultaneously lower the upper back to the mat. As you roll on the back, straddle, reaching between the legs to push off hands to a straddle stand.

2 **Scale to Forward Roll** From a front scale, lift the free leg backward and up as the hands are placed on the mat. Push off the supporting foot and execute a forward roll to a stand.

3 **Forward Roll Series** During the first forward roll, the body should be at a right angle pike position when rolling on the back. On the second forward roll, elevate to an inverted upper back balance.

FORWARD ROLLING OVER SKILLS

Level of Difficulty: B

4 Handstand Position to Forward Roll (shown with a spot)
Push off one leg and swing the other to handstand position. From the handstand position, continue to forward roll with extended arms to a stand. (It is recommended that a spotter be used to assist with the handstand into a forward roll.)

> *What to practice:*
> - Move through a lunge to place hands on the floor.
> - Support body weight on hands during the roll.
> - Continue forward motion all the way up to a stand.

5 Steps to Handstand to Forward Roll Step-Out Take two or three steps with the arms high. Push with one leg and swing the other leg toward the handstand position. Continue to forward roll with extended arms to a step-out. (It is recommended that a spotter be used to assist with the handstand into a forward roll.)

6 Lunge to Handstand to Forward Roll (shown with a spot)
From a lunge position, lever to handstand position. Then, lower to upper back with extended legs and continue to forward roll (It is recommended that a spotter be used to assist with the handstand into a forward roll.)

FORWARD ROLLING OVER SKILLS

Level of difficulty: C

7 **Two Foot Push Squat to Handstand to Forward Roll** Push off two feet to handstand position. Overbalance the handstand, then lower to upper back with extended legs and continue to the forward roll.

8 **Straddle or Pike Push to Handstand Forward Roll** From a straddle or pike stand, push off both feet to handstand position. Then, lower to upper back and continue the forward roll.

9 **Handstand Forward Roll Series** Swing leg to handstand forward roll, then squat push to handstand roll. Pike or straddle push to handstand roll.

What to practice:
- Keep arms straight in handstand position.
- Roll forward onto the upper back.
- Maintain control throughout.

I CAN DO GYMNASTICS

BACKWARD ROLLING SKILLS WITH A WEDGE OR STACKED MATS

Level of difficulty: A

1 **Back Roll Down with Basic Body Positions** From a stand on the high end of the wedge, backward roll (with hands placed on mat by ears) to a stand showing various basic body positions. (Tuck, pike, straddled and/or combinations).

2 Repeat skill number one with extended arms. (*Hint: Turn hands inward so that the fingers of both hands point to each other.*)

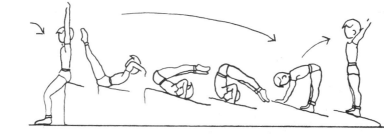

3 **Straddle, Pike Backward Roll to a Stand** From a stand on the floor mat, sit on the high end of a wedge and execute a back roll to a straddle stand.

BACKWARD ROLLING SKILLS WITH A WEDGE OR STACKED MATS

Level of difficulty: B

4 **Pike Backward Roll** Repeat skill number three with legs together.

5 **Cartwheel, Backward Roll Down the Wedge** From a lunge facing the high end of the wedge, cartwheel to a stand on both feet onto the floor mat (back to wedge). Sit on the high end of the wedge and execute a backward roll down the wedge. (Show various body positions.)

What to practice:

- Show rhythm in cartwheel.
- Support body weight on hands during backward roll.
- Maintain continuous movement throughout series.

6 **Back Extension Roll To Step-out** From a stand on the floor, sit on the high end of the wedge and backward roll with extension of the body to a 45° handstand or higher and step-out to a lunge.

BACKWARD ROLLING SKILLS WITH A WEDGE OR STACKED MATS

Level of difficulty: C

7 **Back Extension to Near Handstand, Forward Roll to Lie on Mat** From a stand on the floor mat, sit on the high end of the wedge and back roll with extension of the body to a "near" (short of vertical) handstand forward. Roll out of this position to lie on the wedge.

8 **Back Extension Roll to Handstand Step-out** Repeat skill number six, but the step-out is not initiated until the body has passed through momentary handstand.

> *What to practice:*
> - Roll backward with back rounded.
> - Hips and shoulders extend simultaneously.
> - Step-out onto flexed leg.

9 **Back Extension Roll With Extended Arms** Repeat skill number eight, keeping the arms extended (straight) and lower the body through the handstand position to land with control.

BACKWARD ROLLING OVER SKILLS

Level of difficulty: A

1 **Straddle Backward Roll** From a straddle stand, sit back placing the hands between the legs. Execute a backward roll in the straddled pike position to a straddle stand.

2 **Pike Backward Roll** From a stand, pike forward and sit back with straight legs. Execute a backward roll in pike to a stand.

3 **Backward Roll Series** Tuck back roll, straddle back roll, and piked back roll.

What to practice:

- Use the arms and hand placement to protect the head and neck.
- Build momentum in the sit-back to assist the turnover.
- Maintain weight on the arms and hands until balance is achieved on the feet.

BACKWARD ROLLING OVER SKILLS

Level of difficulty: B

4 **Back Extension to Arabesque (both legs)** Execute a back extension roll with a step-out to arabesque.

5 **Back Extension, Snap Down** Execute a back extension roll to a handstand, snap-down to a stand.

6 **Back Extension, Handstand, Step-out** Execute a back extension roll to a handstand. Step-out to front scale (hold two or three counts).

BACKWARD ROLLING OVER SKILLS

Level of difficulty: C

7 **Back Extension, Forward Roll** Execute a back extension roll to a handstand. Roll out of a handstand forward to a stand.

8 **Back Extension, Bridge** Execute a back extension roll to a handstand. Limber over to a momentary bridge.

9 **Back Extension Series** Combine three back extensions into one series (may show various body positions).

INVERTED BALANCE SKILLS

Level of difficulty: A

1 **Handstand Roll-out From Wall Support**

2 **Lift to Momentary Handstand (shown with a spot)** Swing one leg to the inverted position while pushing with the other leg. Support your weight on your hands with the body extended. A spotter should be used at the back or upper legs.

3 **Lift to Momentary Handstand** Swing one leg to inverted position while pushing with the other leg. Support your weight on your hands with the body and arms extended. Keep the legs in the stride position so your balance will not be disturbed.

INVERTED BALANCE SKILLS

Level of difficulty: B

4 **Lift to Momentary Handstand** Repeat skill number three with feet pulled together.

> *What to practice:*
> - Perform entire series slowly and with control.
> - Place arms on mat with the elbows extended.
> - Bring legs together slowly after balance has been achieved.

5 **Lift to Handstand** Repeat skill number four and hold for two seconds.

6 **Cartwheel to Handstand** Slow push through the cartwheel position. Stop in the handstand position and hold for one second then slowly lower down to one foot.

I CAN DO GYMNASTICS

INVERTED BALANCE SKILLS

Level of difficulty: C

7 **Handstand 90° Turn** From the handstand position, slowly shift the weight to one hand. With the other hand, walk to a 90° handstand hold.

8 **Handstand 180° Turn** From the handstand position shift weight to one hand walking to a 90° turn, then shift the other hand back 90°, to make a 180° turn.

> *What to practice:*
> - Maintain stretched body position.
> - Shift weight using shoulder shrugs.
> - Move slowly and with control.

9 **Straddle or Squat Flexed Arm Press to Handstand** From either position (straddle or squat) shift the weight off the feet forward to hands with the hips aligned over the shoulders. Use the strength in the upper and lower back to lift the body off the floor to an arm support. When balance on the hands has been achieved, raise the legs upward to a handstand.

INVERTED AGILITY SKILLS (CARTWHEELS)

Level of difficulty: A

1 **Three Steps, Cartwheel** Stand with the arms elevated over the head. Step left then right then push off the left foot to a cartwheel.

2 **Step, Hurdle, Cartwheel** Stand with the arms above the head. Lower the arms, swinging them back and step (left or right). While pushing off the step-leg, swing arms forward to hurdle (skip step) on other leg. Step on original leg with arms reaching forward and push to a cartwheel.

3 **Cartwheel to Run-out Backward** Run and hurdle to a cartwheel facing forward (1/4 turn) and continue to run backward.

What to practice:
- Push off flexed leg into cartwheel.
- Exaggerate arm push to over-rotate landing.
- Run backward upon landing to continue momentum.

INVERTED AGILITY SKILLS (CARTWHEELS)

Level of difficulty: B

4 **Cartwheel to Forward Run-out** Run and hurdle to a cartwheel facing forward (1/4 turn) and continue to run forward.

5 **One-arm Cartwheel** Stand push to a near arm cartwheel, taking the far arm through without touching the mat.

6 **Cartwheel Spring-out** Step and swing left leg hard to left body. Push vigorously with arms and shoulder and continue the cartwheel. Be sure to show flight from the push off of the hands to the landing of the feet.

INVERTED AGILITY SKILLS (CARTWHEELS)

Level of difficulty: C

7 **Cartwheel Series Walking** Step and push into a cartwheel. As the second leg lands, push to the next cartwheel and continue.

8 **Cartwheel Chassé Cartwheel Series** Step and push into a cartwheel. Step out, pull feet together with arms elevated (chassé), then push to the next cartwheel.

9 **Cartwheels Accelerated** Repeat skill number seven, but increase the speed of each cartwheel up to three or four cartwheels.

What to practice:

- Accelerate cartwheels gradually.
- Flex arms and legs when contacting the floor to assist with push.
- Maintain a straight line floor path.

INVERTED AGILITY SKILLS (ROUND-OFFS)

Level of difficulty: A

1 **Cartwheel-style Round-off** Step and push through cartwheel position. Upon landing, close the back foot to the front foot.

2 **Step Into Round-off** Step facing forward with shoulders squared. Push with the step leg and lift the hips, then the extending leg. Reach forward with the first hand to the mat and then over-reach with the second hand. This vertical push ensures that the body will rotate and elevate. When both hands are on the mat, turn and face backward. While vertical, push vigorously so a snap-down can be accomplished.

3 **Three Steps to a Round-off** Take three steps and repeat skill number two. If the push is to be done with the left leg, the first step must be on the left leg.

INVERTED AGILITY SKILLS (ROUND-OFFS)

Level of difficulty: B

4 **Step Hurdle to Round-off** Step, hurdle, push and repeat skill number two.

> *What to practice:*
> * Flex front leg on hurdle in preparation for push-off.
> * Push vigorously with arms for snap-down.
> * Pull legs through to flexed landing, leaning slightly backwards.

5 **Power Hurdle to Round-off** From a stand, jump forward and swing arm to reach forward. If you are a left tumbler, land on the right leg first as though performing a hurdler. After landing on the right leg, push with the left leg to a round-off. After landing, flex legs upon landing and elevate to vertical position to prepare for future tumbling.

6 **Power Hurdle to Round-off to Straddle Jump** Repeat skill number five, land leaning slightly forward to be able to punch to a straddle jump.

INVERTED AGILITY SKILLS (ROUND-OFFS)

Level of difficulty: C

7 **Power Hurdle to Round-off to Cartwheel** Repeat skill number five, but change the body's alignment to punch to cartwheel.

8 **Handstand, Step-down, Cartwheel, Round-off** From a handstand position, lower down to the right leg (if a left handed tumbler). Push to the left leg with a 180° turn and continue to a round-off.

9 **Round-off Punch Cartwheel to Round-off** Run, hurdle to round-off, punch to cartwheel to immediate round-off.

What to practice:

- Travel in a straight line path.
- Move quickly with control.
- Accelerate final round-off to run backward.
- Arms raise above the head between all skills.

WALKOVER DEVELOPMENT DRILLS

Level of Difficulty: A

1 Kneeling, Sitting on Heels and Reach Back Close to a Wall.

2 Kneeling on Heels and Reach Back to a Wall Farther Away from a Wall.

3 Upright Kneeling Reaching Backward Close to a Wall.

WALKOVER DEVELOPMENT DRILLS

Level of Difficulty: B

4 Upright Kneeling Reaching Backward Farther Away from a Wall.

5 Standing and Reaching Back to a Wall Close to a Wall.

6 Standing and Reaching Back to a Wall Farther Away from a Wall.

WALKOVER DEVELOPMENT DRILLS

Level of Difficulty: C

7

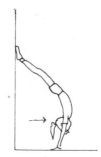

Hyper-flexing in a Handstand Against a Wall.

8

Lever to Handstand Front Limber to Momentary Bridge.

9

Tic-Toc Between Two Stacked Mats.

CHECKLIST FOR TUMBLING SKILLS AND SEQUENCES

Skill	Level of Difficulty			Date Skill Series Completed
	A	B	C	
Upright Balance Skills				
Balancing Strength Skills				
Upright Agility Skills				
Forward Rolling Skills (with Stacked Mats or Wedge)				
Forward Rolling Over Skills				
Backward Rolling Skills (with Stacked Mats or Wedge)				
Backward Rolling Over Skills				
Inverted Balance Skills				
Inverted Agility Skills (Cartwheels)				
Inverted Agility Skills (Round-offs)				
Walkover Development Drills				

5

Vaulting Skills and Sequences

SQUAT VAULTING SKILLS

Level of difficulty: A

1 **Front Leaning Support to Squat** From a front leaning support position on the floor, bring the knees forward to squat position while shifting the weight to the hands. Return to front leaning support position.

2 **Squat from Extended Body with Feet Elevated** From front leaning position with feet elevated on a folded panel mat, bring knees forward to a squat position on base mat. Continue to support weight on the hands and come to a stand.

3 **Squat on Mats, Jump Off** With folded panel mats and a spring-board placed close together, place hands on top of the mats and stand on springboard. Bounce several times and squat to top of mats. Immediately jump off mats to a stand.

SQUAT VAULTING SKILLS

Level of difficulty: B

4 **Walk to Squat on Mats, Jump Off** With two folded panel mats and a springboard placed close together, move forward with several running steps. Rebound with a two-foot takeoff and vault to a squat position on top of the mats. Immediately jump off the mats to a stand.

5 **Run to Squat on Two Mats, Jump Off** With two folded panel mats and a springboard placed close together, move forward with several running steps. Rebound with a two-foot takeoff and vault to a squat position on top of mats. Immediately jump off mats to a stand.

What to practice:
- Show arm support prior to squat.
- Jump upward and forward with control.
- Land in demi-plié.

6 **Run to Squat on Three Mats, Jump Off** With three folded panel mats and a springboard placed close together, move forward with several running steps. Rebound with a two-foot takeoff and vault to squat position on top of the mats. Immediately jump off mats to a stand.

Note: Make sure mats stacked three high are stable. If not, use a vaulting trapezoid or a gymnastics vaulting horse adjusted to the appropriate height.

SQUAT VAULTING SKILLS

Level of difficulty: C

Note: Make sure mats stacked three high are stable. If not, use a vaulting trapezoid or a gymnastics vaulting horse adjusted to the appropriate height.

7 **Squat Vault** With three folded panel mats and a springboard placed close together, move forward with several running steps. Rebound with a two-foot takeoff and squat vault over the mats to land in demi-plié with back to mats.

8 **Stretched Squat Vault** With three folded panel mats and a springboard placed close together, move forward with several running steps. Rebound with a two-foot takeoff and squat vault over the mats to land in demi-plié with back to mats. (Be sure to show an extended body position in the flight to the stacked mats)

9 **Squat-Open Vault** With three folded panel mats and a springboard placed close together, move forward with several running steps. Rebound with a two-foot takeoff and squat vault over mats. Extend body prior to landing in demi-plié with back to mats in an SLP.

STRADDLE VAULTING

Level of difficulty: A

1 Leap Frog Stand at one end of a folded panel mat. Place hands on the mat and face the other end. Push on mat as you straddle legs to move up and over the mat. Land with the legs together at the end of the mat, arms in front of the body.

Note: This skill can also be performed over another person. Place your hands on the lower back of your partner, push and straddle over to land in front of your partner's head.

2 Front Leaning Support to Straddle From a front leaning support position on the floor, bring the legs forward to a straddle position while shifting your weight to your hands. Return to a front leaning support position.

3 Straddle from Extended Body Position with Feet Elevated From a front leaning position with feet elevated on a folded panel mat, bring legs forward to a straddle position on a base mat while supporting your weight on your hands. Come to a stand.

STRADDLE VAULTING

Level of difficulty: B

4 Bounce to Straddle Sit With a springboard placed close to a trapezoid turned long-ways, bounce from a stand on the board and jump to a seated straddle position with a two-hand support between the legs.

5 Walk, Bounce to Straddle Sit With a springboard placed close to a trapezoid turned long-ways, walk and jump on the board to the seated straddle position with a two-hand support.

6 Walk, Bounce to Straddle Sit, Push to Landing With a springboard placed close to a trapezoid turned long-ways, walk and jump off the board to a seated straddle position with two-hand support. After arriving at seated position push with hands to a stand on the mat at the far end of trapezoid.

What to practice:
- Keep hips and legs low in preflight.
- Push with the arms to lean backward to straddle seat.
- Swing legs forward and push to a stand.

STRADDLE VAULTING

Level of Difficulty: C

7 **Low Straddle Vault** With a springboard placed close to a trapezoid turned long-ways, run and jump on the board and vault with legs low to two-hand support in straddle position to land with feet together in demi-plié.

8 **Stretched Straddle Vault** With a springboard placed close to a trapezoid turned long-ways, run and jump on the board and vault with hips at or slightly above horizontal and legs below to two-hand support in the straddle position to land with feet together in demi-plié.

9 **Straddle-Open Vault** With a springboard placed close to a trapezoid turned long-ways, run and jump on the board and vault to an extended position in the afterflight prior to landing with the feet together in demi-plié.

FRONT/SIDE VAULTING SKILLS

Level of difficulty: A

1 **Tuck Round-off** With springboard placed close to panel mats stacked two high (sideways), bounce on the board and vault over the panel mats in tucked position with two-hand support turning toward the mats on descent. Land in a stand facing the mat.

2 **Pike Round-off** With the springboard placed close to the panel mats stacked two high (sideways), bounce on the board and vault over the panel mats in a piked position with two-hand support, turn 180° toward mats on descent. Land in a stand facing the mat.

3 **Pike to Extension Round-off** With springboard placed close to panel mats stacked two high (sideways), bounce on the board and vault over panel mats in a pike position, with two-hand support stretching and extending body while turning toward mats on descent. Land in a stand facing the mat.

FRONT/SIDE VAULTING SKILLS

Level of difficulty: B

4 **Tucked Cartwheel with 1/4 Turn Outward** With the springboard placed close to panel mats stacked two high (sideways), bounce on the board and vault over the panel mats in tucked position with two-hand support. Execute a 1/4 turn away from the mat on descent. Land in a stand with the back facing the mat.

5 **Piked Cartwheel** With a springboard placed close to the panel mats stacked two high (sideways), bounce on the board and vault over panel mat in piked position with two-hand support executing a 1/4 turn away from mat on descent. Land in a stand with the back facing the mat.

6 **Cartwheel with 1/4 Turn Outward** With springboard placed close to panel mats stacked two high (sideways), bounce on the board and vault over panel mat with two-hand support. Execute a 1/4 turn away from mat on descent. Land in a stand with the back facing the mat.

FRONT/SIDE VAULTING SKILLS

Level of difficulty: C

7 **Tucked Front Handspring** With springboard placed close to panel mats stacked two high (sideways), rebound off the board and vault over the panel mats in a tuck position with two-hand support. Land in a stand with back facing mat.

8 **Piked Front Handspring** With springboard placed close to panel mats stacked two high (sideways), rebound off the board and vault over the panel mats in a piked position with two-hand support. Land in a stand with back facing the mat.

9 **Front Handspring** With a springboard placed close to panel mats stacked two high (sideways), rebound off the board and vault over panel mats in piked position with two-hand support. Land in a stand with back to mats.

CHECKLIST FOR VAULTING SKILLS AND SEQUENCES

Skill	Level of Difficulty			Date Skill Series Completed
	A	B	C	
Squat Vaulting				
Straddle Vaulting				
Front/Side Vaulting				

6

Beam Skills and Sequences

MOUNTS WITH BEAM AT HIP HEIGHT

Level of difficulty: A

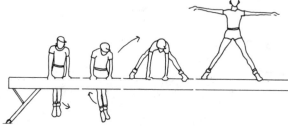

1 **Front Support to Straddle** From a front support position on the side of the beam, swing legs backward and upward while piking in the hips. Place feet on the beam outside hands in a straddle support. Rise to straddle stand.

2 **Step Up to Balance Stand** With the springboard positioned at the end of the beam, take two or three steps to push off one foot onto the top of the beam. Pass through a low arabesque to stand on both feet. (You may also perform this mount from a stand on the springboard or floor.)

What to practice:

- Use arms to assist with jump.
- Maintain eye contact with the beam.
- Control upper body movements.

3 **Jump to Balance Stand** From two or three steps or a stand on the springboard (or floor), jump from two feet to land on the end of the beam with slightly flexed knees (demi-plié).

MOUNTS WITH BEAM AT HIP HEIGHT

Level of difficulty: B

4 **Scissors Mount** Start diagonally from one side of the beam. Stand or walk on springboard (or floor) and place inside hand on the top of the beam and step off the opposite leg. Lift the leg next to the beam up and over the beam. Follow this leg immediately with the push-off leg. Land in a side sitting position with one hand on the beam behind the body (legs on the opposite side of the beam from which you started.)

5 **Squat Mount** From a stand facing the side of the beam on the springboard (or floor), place hands on the top of the beam and jump to place both feet on top of the beam between your hands. Lift arms to optional position with erect torso.

6 **Straddle Mount** From a stand facing the side of the beam on the springboard (or floor), place both hands on top of the beam and jump to a straddle stand with both feet on top of the beam outside hands with straight legs.

MOUNTS WITH BEAM AT HIP HEIGHT

Level of difficulty: C

7 **Wolf Mount** Stand facing the side of the beam. Place hands on top of the beam and jump (from springboard or floor) to arrive on top of beam. Bend one leg to place the foot between the hands. Lift the straight leg to the side and place it on the beam to the outside of the hands (in a side lunge).

8 **Straddle "L" Turn** Facing the end of the beam with hands near the end, jump and straddle the legs while simultaneously turning the body 180° with the support of the arms. During the turn, one leg is lifted over the beam to finish in a cross straddle seat (arms optional).

9 **Pullover Mount** From a stand, undergrip and walk under the beam. Push off the floor with one leg while lifting the other leg over and around the beam. Pull beam toward waist and rotate backward over the beam (execute as for single bar skill).

LOCOMOTOR/STATIC COMBINATIONS

1 **Front Attitude, Step Hop, Chassé, Assemblé** From a stand on the beam, with the free leg in front attitude position (moving forward), step-hop, chassé, assemblé. Show a variety of arm positions.

STEPS

- R-R Step-hop
- L-R-L Chassé
- L-R Assemblé (or reverse)

2 **Scale, Chassé, Hitchkick** Stand on the beam and execute a front scale. Lift the torso, step forward and chassé. From the chassé, hitchkick and step forward to finish in an extended stand. (Arms optional.)

STEPS

- R Scale
- L-R-L Chassé
- Push L, land R Hitchkick
- Step L (or reverse)

Note: All of the basic locomotor skills are shown in I Can Do Gymnastics: Essential Skills for Beginning Gymnasts. *These are various combinations. Suggested steps are indicated.*

LOCOMOTOR/STATIC COMBINATIONS

Note: All of the basic locomotor skills are shown in I Can Do Gymnastics: Essential Skills for Beginning Gymnasts. *These are various combinations. Suggested steps are indicated.*

3 Two Dip-Steps, Chassé, Stride Leap, and Step to Stand

From a stand on the beam, step forward two dip-steps, chassé, stride leap and land through a low arabesque. Finish by stepping forward into an extended stand with the rear foot pointed behind the body on the beam. (Arms optional.)

STEPS

- Step L (dip)
- Step R (dip)
- L-R-L Chassé
- Push L, land R (leap)
- Step L (or reverse)

4 Cat Leap, Hitchkick
Stand on beam, step forward into a cat leap, step, hitchkick, step to finish in an extended stand with the rear foot pointed behind the body on the beam (arms optional). (The elements can be reversed.)

STEPS

- Step (push) L, land R (cat leap)
- Step (push) L, land R (hitchkick)
- Step L, finish (or reverse)

LOCOMOTOR/STATIC COMBINATIONS

Note: All of the basic locomotor skills are shown in I Can Do Gymnastics: Essential Skills for Beginning Gymnasts. *These are various combinations. Suggested steps are indicated.*

5 **Step, Hop, Kick, Step, Stretch Jump** Stand on the beam and step, hop, step, kick to horizontal. Close free leg to place the foot slightly in front of the other foot in demi-plié. Immediately stretch jump to land in demi-plié and extend to a stand. (Arms optional.)

STEPS

- Step L, land L, (hop)
- Step R, kick L (close in front)
- Jump from both to land on both (or reverse)

6 **Stretch Jump, Tuck Jump** Stand on the beam with one foot in front of the other, demi-plié and stretch jump. Land on the beam in a demi-plié and immediately push off the beam with both feet to perform a tuck jump. Land on the beam in demi-plié with one foot in front of the other. Extend to a stand, arms optional. (The second jump may be a squat jump.)

LOCOMOTOR/STATIC COMBINATIONS

Note: All of the basic locomotor skills are shown in I Can Do Gymnastics: Essential Skills for Beginning Gymnasts. *These are various combinations.*

7 **Chassé , Chassé , Step, Turn, Lunge** From a stand sideways on the beam, execute two consecutive side chassés. Step sideways, 1/4 turn toward your lead foot, flexing the knee slightly, and keeping the trailing foot extended behind the body with the weight centered over the front foot (lunge).

8 **Tuck Jump, Pivot Turn, Lunge** Stand on the beam with one foot in front of the other, demi-plié, tuck jump, land in demi-plié with one foot in front of the other. Immediately lower your body to squat position and pivot turn 180°. Rise to standing lunge position by extending the rear leg behind (or taking a half step forward) and center your weight over front leg.

9 **Lunge, Squat, Pivot Turn, Stretch Jump, Lunge** Stand on the beam in lunge position. Close the rear foot behind the front foot and lower to a squat position. Pivot turn 180° and push off the beam and execute a stretch jump and land in demi-plié with one foot in front of the other. Rise to a standing lunge by extending the rear leg behind (or taking a half step forward) and center your weight over the flexed front leg.

TUMBLING / NON-LOCOMOTOR / STATIC COMBINATIONS

Level of difficulty: A

1 Piqué Turns Stand on the beam with one foot in front of the other. Step forward onto the ball of the right foot. Turn 180° to the right and bring the left foot to touch the right ankle (piqué position). Step forward on to the ball of the left foot. Turn 180° to the left bringing the right foot to touch the left ankle (piqué position).

2 Scale, Pivot Turns to Passé Stand on the beam and lift one leg upward and to the rear into scale position. Lift torso, step forward and pivot turn 180°. Finish with weight on your front foot and immediately bring up rear foot to touch the knee of the supporting leg in passé position. (Arms optional.)

3 Pivot Turn, Back Attitude, Pivot Turn, Front Attitude Stand on the beam with one foot in front of the other foot and execute 180° pivot turn. Lift rear leg, flexing the knee to back attitude position. Lower leg and step forward. Execute a 180° pivot turn, finishing with weight on the back foot. Lift front leg (with knee flexed) to front attitude position, arms optional.

TUMBLING / NON-LOCOMOTOR / STATIC COMBINATIONS

Level of difficulty: B

4 Shin Scale, Roll Back to Shoulder Balance Stand in a lunge on the beam then lower to a deep lunge. Place hands on the beam in front of the flexed knee and lower to a shin scale then to a saddle sit. Swing the legs forward and together while raising legs to 45°. Roll back to shoulder balance with the hands gripping the beam behind the neck.

5 Backward Roll to Low Lunge through to V-sit from a straddle sit on the beam, roll over backward (hands placed on the beam behind the neck) and pull feet up and over head while pushing with hands on beam to finish in a low lunge position. Place your hands on the beam in front of the forward foot, push off feet to momentary clear straddle. Lower to swing legs forward and up to finish in a V-sit, with hands placed on the beam behind the hips. (The above sequence is an example of one way to get into and out of a backward roll.)

6 Curtsey Pivot Turn, Scale, Shin-Balance Stand on the beam, step forward into a low curtsey. Extend and execute a 180° pivot turn. Lower your weight to the rear leg and swing front leg downward, backward and up to show a forward scale on flexed support leg. Lift torso, place foot of rear leg on beam behind support leg and lower to shin to show a pose.

TUMBLING / NON-LOCOMOTER / STATIC COMBINATIONS

Level of difficulty: C

7 Scale, 90° Turn, Lunge, 90° Turn, Body Wave Stand on the beam and execute a front scale. Lift the torso and step forward with a 90° turn outward into a deep side lunge. Execute another 90° turn in the same direction and close the foot of the extended leg in front of the other foot. Arrive in a squat position with the arms vertical. Execute a forward body wave and rise to finish in a stand on half toe. Arms optional.

8 Lunge, Forward Roll, Squat Stand on the beam and lower to a lunge. Place hands on the beam in front of flexed knee. Lower upper back to the beam in front of the hands and roll forward over back. As roll continues, bring legs forward to the beam and flex knees into tuck. Continue to lift the trunk and hips to finish in the squat position on the beam, with one foot in front of the other.

9 Forward Roll, Straddle Swing to Squat, Body Wave From a stand, squat and execute a forward roll. As the roll is completed, straddle the legs and swing them rearward. Simultaneously push with the hands as the hips lift and bring the feet onto the beam into a squat position. Stand up and contract body forward and upward to a complete stand (bodywave).

BEAM DISMOUNTS

Level of difficulty: A

Note: All dismounts should be performed onto a safe landing surface with appropriate matting. The students should be familiar with appropriate landing positions.

1 **Stretch Jump** From a stand at the end or side of the beam, jump off to a stretched position in the air. Land in a demi-plié and extend to stand.

2 **Tuck/Squat Jump** From a stand at the end or side of the beam, jump to a tuck/squat position in the air. Land in demi-plié and extend to stand.

3 **Straddle Jump** From a stand, jump off to a straddle jump in the air. Bring legs back together in air to land in demi-plié and extend to stand. You may straddle the legs sideward under the body or forward and upward to show a piked straddle position.

BEAM DISMOUNTS

Level of difficulty: B

Note: All dismounts should be performed onto a safe landing surface with appropriate matting. The students should be familiar with appropriate landing positions.

4 **Swing Up and Over (from a straddle-sit)** From a V-sit, swing the legs downward, backward, and upward while pushing upward off the side of the beam. Lower legs to the side of the beam. Land in demi-plié.

5 **Three-Quarter Handstand Dismount** From a lunge, place hands on the beam and lever to a 3/4 handstand. Push slightly to side with hands and lift the chest while the legs swing back under the body to land in demi-plié. Extend to a stand.

6 **Side Handstand Dismount** From a lunge, reach forward and cartwheel to a near handstand with the legs closed. Lower the body to land in demi-plié facing the beam (hands remain on the beam). Extend to a stand.

What to practice:
- Maintain eye contact with beam.
- Keep arms extended during handstand and dismount.
- Move slowly and with control throughout.

BEAM DISMOUNTS

Level of difficulty: C

Note: All dismounts should be performed onto a safe landing surface with appropriate matting. The students should be familiar with appropriate landing positions.

7 **Step to Cartwheel with 1/4 Turn** From a lunge near the end of the beam, reach forward and place your hands on the beam. Execute a cartwheel with 1/4 turn to land in demi-plié with feet together facing the end of the beam. Extend to a stand.

What to practice:

- Travel in a straight line off the end of the beam.
- Keep the arms straight and shoulders extended throughout.
- Maintain eye contact in the intended direction of the motion.

8 **Side Handstand** From a stand, step forward and cartwheel up to a handstand. Overbalance the body and shift weight to one hand. Execute a 90° turn as the body lowers to land beside the beam in demi-plié with the pivot hand still on the beam. Extend to a stand. It is suggested that the instructor spot this skill during learning.

9 **Round-off Dismount** From a lunge near the end of the beam, reach forward and place your hands on the beam. Execute a round-off with repulsion from the hands and stretched body position in flight to land facing the end of the beam in demi-plié. Extend to a stand.

I CAN DO GYMNASTICS

CHECKLIST FOR BALANCE BEAM SKILLS AND SEQUENCES

Skill	Level of Difficulty			Date Skill Series Completed
	A	B	C	
Mounts				
Locomotor/Static Combinations				
Tumbling / Non-Locomotor/ Static Combinations				
Dismounts				

7

Low Bar Skills and Sequences

CIRCLING THE BAR BACKWARD

Level of difficulty: A

1 Back Hip Circle with Flexed Legs From a front support, cast to horizontal. When re-contacting the bar, shift the shoulders backward and flex at the hips. Legs are flexed to facilitate rotation (to shorten the radius of the circle) backward around the bar.

2 Piked Back Hip Circle with Extended Legs From a front support, cast to horizontal. When re-contacting bar, shift the shoulders backward and flex at the hips (pike). Keep legs extended while rotating around the bar backward.

3 Back Hip Circle with Extended Body From a front support, cast to horizontal. When re-contacting the bar, keep body extended while rotating backward around the bar. Body should be in the hollow (chest-pike) position throughout this skill.

I CAN DO GYMNASTICS

CIRCLING THE BAR BACKWARD

Level of difficulty: B

4 Cast to 45° Above Horizontal From a front support, flex at the hips with shoulders forward. Cast (hip extension) legs upward to 45° above the horizontal with extended arms and return to the bar before flexing the hips to maintain control and balance.

5 Extended Body Back Hip Circle from High Cast From a front support, cast to 45° above the horizontal with extended arms. When re-contacting the bar, shift the shoulders backward to generate enough force to circle the bar with an extended body.

What to practice:
- Hips and shoulders extend simultaneously on cast.
- Hands rotate smoothly around the bar.
- Entire movement is continuous.

6 Clear Back Hip Pullover From a step, overgrip the bar and push off the floor with one leg while lifting the other leg in front of and around the bar. Pull the bar toward the waist without allowing the waist to touch the bar. Shift the wrists backward while rotating backward around the bar.

Low Bar Skills and Sequences

CIRCLING THE BAR BACKWARD

Level of difficulty: C

7 **Jump to Back Hip Circle (flexed hips or hollow body)** From a folded mat, jump to a momentary front support to a back hip circle.

8 **Folded Mat Jump to Clear Back Hip Circle** From a folded mat, jump to a front support position. Before arriving in the front support, shift the shoulders backward. Maintain the extended body position while rotating around the bar backward without touching the bar (except with the hands).

9 **Clear Back Hip Circle (from high cast)** From a front support, cast 45° above horizontal. Upon returning to the bar, shift the shoulders backward and maintain the extended body position while rotating around the bar backward without touching the bar (except with the hands).

CIRCLING THE BAR FORWARD

Level of difficulty: A

1 Single Knee Up From a single knee hang and using an overgrip, extend the non-hanging leg out and down to generate force to rotate forward, up and above the bar. Finish in a stride support

2 Single Knee Rock Back From a stride support and using an overgrip, rock backward to a single knee swing to a single leg up to stride support.

3 Single Leg Kip From a stride support and using an overgrip, rock back to a stride swing to a single leg kip returning to stride support.

CIRCLING THE BAR FORWARD

Level of difficulty: B

4 **Forward Stride Circle** From a front support, single leg cut to a stride support. Change to an undergrip and extend the front leg. Place the back leg against bar and shift the shoulders forward to circle the bar in stride position. (Spot at wrist and back.)

5 **Jump to Forward Rollover** From a stand on a folded mat, grip the bar with an overgrip and jump, passing through support position. Shift the shoulders forward and shift the grip around to roll forward slowly to a stand.

6 **Forward Rollover** From a front support, shift the shoulders forward to a horizontal extended body position. Slowly roll forward with pike to a stand.

What to practice:

- Arms extended in support.
- Wrists "shift" around the bar during the roll.
- Perform entire skill slowly and with control.

CIRCLING THE BAR FORWARD

Level of difficulty: C

7 **Front Hip Circle (tuck)** From a front support, shift the shoulders forward to horizontal with an extended body position. Then, roll forward with a tucked body and circle the bar tucked.

8 **Front Hip Circle (pike)** From a front support, shift the shoulders forward to horizontal extended body position. Roll forward with a piked body and circle the body forward.

9 **Front Hip Circles** Perform two front hip circles in succession showing open (extended) body position between the two circles.

HIP CASTING TO UNDERSWINGS WITH SOLE CIRCLE

Level of difficulty: A

1 **Jump to Sole Circle and Swing to a Stand** From a standing position on folded panel mats with extended arms and an overgrip, jump and flex hips to a piked straddle position on the bar with feet on bar outside hands. Maintain position, underswing, release, and stand.

2 **Climb to Underswing to a Stand (with spot)** From a front support, climb to a straddle stand on the bar, shift shoulders backward (with spot) and flex at the hips as approaching the downswing. Maintain position until swing is completed, then extend and release to a stand.

3 **Climb to Underswing to a Stand (no spot)** From a front support, climb to a straddle stand on the bar, shift shoulders backward and flex at the hips as approaching downswing. Maintain position until swing is completed, then extend and release to a stand.

HIP CASTING TO UNDERSWINGS WITH SOLE CIRCLE

Level of difficulty: B

4 **Straddle Touch Feet to Bar** From a front support, cast to horizontal. Pike and straddle, touching both feet on the bar, and then return to a stand while holding the bar.

5 **Straddle Stand Jump Dismount (with spot)** From a front support, cast to a horizontal. Pike and straddle, placing both feet on the bar. Shift shoulders forward and then jump off the bar forward to stand in front of the bar.

6 **Straddle Underswing Dismount** From a front support, cast to a piked straddle sole circle. Close pike position on down swing and keep closed until swing is completed. Extend and release bar to a stand.

What to practice:
- Cast with balance and control.
- Place feet on the bar near the hands.
- Land in demi-plié showing control.

HIP CASTING TO UNDERSWINGS WITH SOLE CIRCLE

Level of difficulty: C

7 **Jump Underswing Half-Turn Dismount** From a standing position on a folded mat, jump to a piked straddle sole circle. Close pike position on downswing and keep closed until swing is completed. Extend, release, and execute a half-turn of the body to stand. (Practice turning in both directions.)

8 **Cast Underswing to Half-Turn Dismount** From a front support, cast to a piked straddle sole circle. Close piked position on downswing and keep closed until the swing is completed. Extend, release, and execute a half-turn of the body to stand. (Practice turning in both directions.)

What to practice:
- Extend at the hips and shoulders at the peak of the swing.
- Begin half-turn after release.
- Complete half-turn prior to landing.

9 **Underswing to Half-Turn to Pike Glide** Repeat skill number eight. From the stand, re-grip (overgrip) the bar. Jump to a pike glide. Swing forward and backward, pike swing to a stand. (Practice turning in both directions.)

BELOW BAR SWING TO GLIDE KIP

Level of difficulty: A

1 **Straddled Pike Glide** From a stand with extended arms, jump to an overgrip and swing under the bar in a straddled pike position while keeping feet close to the floor.

2 **Pike Glide** From a stand with extended arms, jump to an overgrip and swing under the bar in pike position, keeping the feet close to the floor.

3 **Straddled Pike Glide and Return to Pike Glide** From a stand with extended arms and overgrip, swing under the bar in a straddled pike glide and swing back piked to a stand.

BELOW BAR SWING TO GLIDE KIP

Level of difficulty: B

4 **Glide, Single Leg in, Swing to Single Knee Up** From a stand with extended arms, jump to an overgrip and swing under the bar in pike position. Extend body and lift single leg between arms (close shoulder angle) to single knee hang, swing again to single knee up.

5 **Glide, Single Leg Kip (single leg overshoot)** From a stand with extended arms, jump to overgrip and swing under the bar in pike position. Extend the body and lift single leg between the arms (close shoulder angle) to single leg kip to stride support.

6 **Short Kip (with spot)** Place folded mats in front of the bar about half the height of the low bar. Sit on mats and reach back to the bar with overgrip. Extend the body and flex at the hips. Immediately close the shoulder angle to kip above the bar while backswing is occurring.

BELOW BAR SWING TO GLIDE KIP

Level of difficulty: C

7 **Short Kip Over Mat** Place folded mats in front of bar about half the height of the low bar. Sit on mats and reach back to the bar with an overgrip. Extend body and flex at the hips, immediately close shoulder angle to kip above the bar while backswing is occurring.

8 **Straddled Pike Glide Kip** From a stand with extended arms, jump to overgrip and swing under the bar in straddled pike position. Pull legs together, extend body at end of swing and flex at hips. Close shoulder angle to kip above the bar.

9 **Glide Kip** From a stand with extended arms, jump to overgrip and swing under the bar in pike position. Extend the body at the end of the swing and flex at the hips. Close shoulder angle to kip above the bar.

What to practice:
- Glide swing is smooth and continuous.
- Keep hips next to the bar while body extends.
- Wrist shift to support position.

ABOVE BAR SWING TO KIP

Level of difficulty: A

1 **Jump, Underswing to Stand** From a stand with extended arms and overgrip, jump and flex at the hips. Bring the ankles close to the bar and hold this position. Swing under the bar and extend body upward and outward. Release grip and come to a stand in front of the bar.

2 **Underswing Forward and Backward to a Stand** From a stand with extended arms and overgrip, jump and immediately flex at the hips, bringing ankles close to the bar. Maintain this position and swing the hips under the bar forward then backward. Extend body upward and release hands. Come to a stand facing the bar.

3 **Drop Underswing Dismount** From a front support, shift the shoulders backward and immediately flex at the hips. Bring the ankles close to the bar while swinging under. Hold this position until the end of the swing. Extend and shoot to a stand.

ABOVE BAR SWING TO KIP

Level of difficulty: B

4 **Drop Underswing Forward and Backward to Stand** From a front support in overgrip, shift the shoulders backward. Immediately, flex at the hips and bring ankles close to the bar. Maintain this position and swing under the bar forward then backward. Release to a stand in back of the bar.

What to practice:
- Pike and lean backward simultaneously.
- Shift wrists on backward swing.
- Release grip at peak of backward swing.

5 **Single Leg Cut, Drop, Single Leg Kip** From a front support, single leg cut, shift shoulders backward and immediately flex at the hips with the front leg. Underswing backward, keeping the front leg away from the bar. Swing back and single leg kip up.

6 **Front Support, Push Away to Glide Swings** From a front support, shift shoulders backward and flex at the hips. The body must be completely extended at the end of the front glide before returning to the backward swing of the glide. Repeat glide swing position to another glide.

ABOVE BAR SWING TO KIP

Level of difficulty: C

7 **Push Away, Glide to Single Knee Up** From a front support, shift shoulders backward and flex at the hips. Glide to an extended body position. On the backswing of the glide, lift one leg to a single knee hang and rock backward to a single knee up.

8 **Push Away to Glide to Single Leg Kip** Repeat skill number seven, but place the single leg between your arms at the end of the glide. Backswing and single leg kip.

> *What to practice:*
> - Push-away is smooth and continuous.
> - Pull with straight legs between the arms.
> - Finish in a stride support.

9 **Drop Under Kip** From a front support, push off balance backward and immediately flex at the hips while keeping ankles close to the bar. Swing through in pike position. At the end of the swing, open slightly to help swing and immediately close to swing back. As soon as the return swing starts, extend at the hips and close the shoulder angle to kip to support.

　　　　　　　I CAN DO GYMNASTICS

SUPPORT BALANCE AND TURNING TO SWING AND KIPS

Level of difficulty: A

1 Single Leg Cut, Turn, Underswing Piked From a front support with an overgrip, single leg cut (left leg) and undergrip with the right hand. Turn right and bring the leg back over to a front support. Re-grip (overgrip) to a rock back piked underswing dismount.

2 Single Leg Over, Turn to a Front Support From a front support, single leg over and undergrip hand on the front leg side. Bring the rear leg over the bar and execute a half-turn with the body arriving in a front support on the bar in the opposite direction.

3 Cuts and Turn to Underswing From a front support, flank the rear leg over the bar and execute a 180° turn toward the undergrip hand to finish in a front support. Immediately drop to an underswing dismount.

SUPPORT BALANCE AND TURNING TO SWING AND KIPS

Level of difficulty: B

4 **Forward and Backward Leg Cuts to Underswing Dismount**
From a front support, single leg cut one leg and then the other leg to a rear support. Execute single leg cuts back to a front support to underswing dismount.

What to practice:
- Shift weight to support arm during leg cuts.
- Cut legs with extended knees.
- Show control on landing.

5 **Forward and Backward Single Leg Cuts to Glide** Repeat skill four but shift the shoulders backward to piked glide.

6 **Forward and Backward Single Leg Cuts with Multiple Glides** Repeat skill number five, but push away from the bar to piked underswing (glide) and repeat glide.

I CAN DO GYMNASTICS

SUPPORT BALANCE AND TURNING TO SWING AND KIPS

Level of difficulty: C

7 **Cut, Turn to Single Knee-up** From a front support, cut one leg over the bar, turn 180°, and bring the other leg over the bar to arrive in a front support.

> *What to practice:*
> - Shift weight to support arm on legs cuts and turns.
> - Show continuous glide motion.
> - Shift wrists to finish in stride support.

8 **Cut, Turn to Single Leg Kip** From a front support, turn, re-grip, and push away from the bar to a glide to single leg kip.

9 **Cut, Turn to Kip or Drop Kip** From a front support, turn, re-grip, push away from the bar to glide kip or shift shoulders backward to a drop kip.

SINGLE LEG SHOOT THROUGH PROGRESSION

Level of difficulty: A

1 Cast, Single Foot on Bar

2 Single Leg Shoot Through (Tucked) to Stride Support

3 Shoot Through with Successively Higher Casts

Note: All previous skills describing a single leg cut may be executed using a shoot through.

DOUBLE LEG SHOOT THROUGH

Level of difficulty: B

1 Similar to single leg through but gymnast must shift shoulders from in front of the bar to behind the bar to finish in a rear support.

CHECKLIST FOR LOW BAR SKILLS AND SEQUENCES

Skill	Level of Difficulty			Date Skill Series Completed
	A	B	C	
Circling the Bar Backward				
Circling the Bar Forward				
Hip Casting to Underswings with Sole Circle				
Below Bar Swing to Glide Kip				
Above Bar Swing to Kip				
Support Balance and Turning to Swing and Kips				
Single Leg Shoot Through Progression				
Double Leg Shoot Though				

I CAN DO GYMNASTICS

8

Advanced Supplement

FLOOR EXERCISES
BACK HANDSPRING PROGRESSIONS

Back Limbers

a Kick over from a bridge with feet on elevated mat.

b Kick over from a bridge on level surface.

c From a stand, backbend to bridge and kick over.

Note: All back or front limbers and other acrobatic flexibility skills such as back and front walkovers should emphasize shoulder flexibility. This permits greater control of the skill(s) and avoids undue stress on the spine.

It is also important for the instructor to emphasize a total curvature of the spine during these skills instead of permitting the student to concentrate the bend in only one portion of the spine, for example, the lower back.

Teaching Hint *When teaching skills that require a backward bending of the spine, encourage the students to periodically rest the back by simply performing a few tucked forward and backward rocking rolls on the mat.*

FLOOR EXERCISES
BACK HANDSPRING PROGRESSIONS

Back Walkovers Sequence

a Back walkover from a stand with forward leg pushing off an elevated mat. Perform first with a spot and then alone. (Shown with three different methods of spotting.)

b Back walkover on a level surface.

Teaching Hint *Because the students tend to learn back and front walkovers on one "preferred" side, it is a good idea to encourage them to make an effort to occasionally perform these skills on the other side and to periodically "rest" the dominant side by simply sitting in the opposite side split for about 45 seconds.*

FLOOR EXERCISES
BACK HANDSPRING PROGRESSIONS

Jump-Back to Stacked Mats or Skill Cushion.

Note: Soft mats are recommended as the students will be landing on their backs. (Slope mats)

a From a stand facing away from waist-high mats or skill cushions, jump-back to sitting or lying position.

> *What to practice:*
> - Strong push-off in cartwheel.
> - Head and arms up with a jump backward.
> - Maintain tight body position when landing.

b Jump-back to stacked mats executed from a cartwheel-type round-off.

c Jump-back to stacked mats or skill cushion from a round-off.

FLOOR EXERCISES
BACK HANDSPRING PROGRESSIONS

Handstand Snapdowns

a Handstand snapdown to landing position with hands on an elevated surface (springboard or folded mat).

b Handstand snapdown with immediate rebound to land lying on back or sitting on a waist-high skill cushion.

Teaching Hint *This is a very important skill requiring timing, coordination, and upperbody strength. A good snapdown should be considered a prerequisite for skills such as the back handspring (flic-flac) or round-off.*

FLOOR EXERCISES
BACK HANDSPRING PROGRESSIONS

Back Handsprings (Flic-Flac - FF)

a With a spot, standing back handspring (FF) to a controlled landing position.

b With a spot, standing back handspring to jump-back to land lying or sitting on a waist high skill cushion. (Used to teach the FF as a connecting skill.)

What to practice:

- Back handspring is smooth and continuous.
- Strong push off the arms.
- Tight legs on jump, slightly flexed.

c Standing back handspring with step-out to lunge position.

Teaching Hint *The back handspring (FF) is a very important tumbling skills. The teacher needs to be aware that the back handspring is used in three different ways and that the techniques used for these are quite different.*

FF to a controlled landing *This technique is utilized when first teaching the FF, and on the balance beam with step-out.*

FF as a connective skill into other skills where the purpose is to generate or maintain horizontal velocity *For example, a series of FFs. In this instance, the student must use a technique that will permit landing off-balance (backward) in a "ready" position to execute the next skill. This is the purpose of the second drill above.*

FF as a transition skill that permits the gymnast to convert horizontal momentum to vertical lift *For example, round-off, FF, back salto. Since back and front saltos are not included at this level of* I Can Do Gymnastics, *this more advanced technique is not discussed here.*

FLOOR EXERCISES
BACK HANDSPRING PROGRESSIONS

Skills into Back Handsprings

a Cartwheel-type round-off into back handspring.

b Cartwheel step-down into back handspring.

c Round-off into back handspring.

Teaching Hint *Similar to the back handspring (FF), the round-off is used in two very different ways.*

A single skill to a controlled landing *The primary use is with beginners or for teaching the round-off as a dismount from the balance beam.*

In tumbling activities. *However, the round-off is used primarily as a skill to convert forward momentum (the run) into backward momentum (usually a FF). In this instance, the student must learn to over-rotate the landing of the round-off so as to be in the best position possible to continue or build horizontal velocity into the next skill.*

Therefore, to encourage good technique, it is suggested that once the students have mastered the basic mechanics of a controlled round-off, they ALWAYS be encouraged to perform at least one FF after the round-off. Obviously, this requires achievement of a good FF as a prerequisite.

FLOOR EXERCISES
BACK HANDSPRING PROGRESSIONS

Skills Out of Round-off-Back Handsprings

a Round-off, Back Handspring, Back Handspring, Step Out.

What to practice:
- Front knee flexed on lunge into round-off.
- Strong arm push off floor throughout.
- Finish in lunge with head and arms high.

b Round-off, Back Handspring, Rebound (Jump) to Land Lying on Back on High Stacked Mats or Skill Cushions.

UNEVEN BARS

Mounts

HB = high bar

LB = low bar

1 **Jump to Swing (HB)** From a stand or run to board, jump to a long swing on the HB facing the LB.

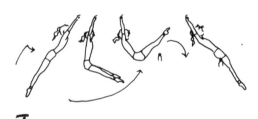

2 **Jump to Swing (HB) and Straddle Over (LB)** From a stand or run to the board, jump to a long swing on the HB facing the LB. On the backswing, flex at the hips and pike (straddle) over the LB to a rear lying hang. *Variation: Jump to a long swing on the HB facing the LB and immediately straddle over the LB to rear lying hang (no intermediate swing).*

UNEVEN BARS

Mounts

3 **Jump to Swing (HB) with Half-Turn (forward)** From a stand or run to the board, jump to a long swing on the HB. On the forward swing, execute a 180° forward turn to a mixed grip.

Grip variations:

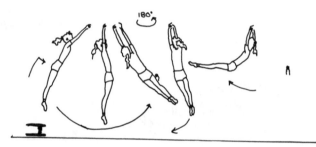

- Double overgrip to mixed grip.

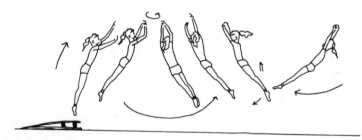

- Mixed grip (release undergrip hand) to another mixed grip.

UNEVEN BARS

Mounts

4 **Jump to Swing (HB) with a 180° turn (backward)** From a stand or run to the board, jump to a long swing on HB with undergrip. On the forward swing, execute a 180° backward turn. (Finish with a swing backward in overgrip.)

5 **Low Bar Mounts**

These skills are illustrated in Chapter seven.

- Pullover.
- Single leg kip (overshoot).

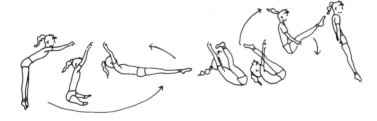

- Double leg overshoot (back-kip).
- Glide kip.

UNEVEN BARS

Mounts

6 **HB/LB combination mounts** From a stand or run to the board, jump to a long swing on HB, immediately...

a Lift (pike) one leg over LB to arrive in a stride hang position.

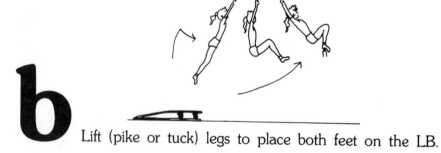

b Lift (pike or tuck) legs to place both feet on the LB.

UNEVEN BARS

Mounts

c Lift both legs over LB: one in tuck and the other in pike. Place the foot of the tucked leg on the LB.

d Lift both legs over LB (tuck or piked) and immediately execute a 180° turn (roll) over hips maintaining a grip on HB with one hand and releasing the other hand during the turn to re-grasp the LB in an overgrip.

UNEVEN BARS

Between Bar Skills

1 Stemrises

a **Single Leg Stemrise** From a rear lying hang position with one leg flexed and the foot on the LB, flex (pike) the extended leg to bring the ankle near the HB. Perform a kipping action while extending and pushing off the LB with the flexed leg. Finish in a front support on the HB facing the LB.

b **Double Leg Stemrise** From a start position hanging on the HB and facing the LB with both legs flexed (tucked) and the feet on the LB, perform a kipping action while extending both legs and pushing off the LB to finish in a front support on the HB facing LB.

I CAN DO GYMNASTICS

UNEVEN BARS

Between Bar Skills

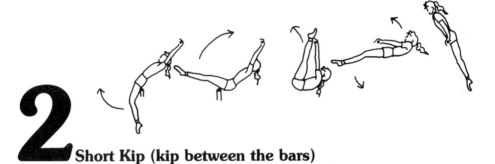

2 Short Kip (kip between the bars)

What to practice:

- Move hips toward bar when extending.
- Pull with extended arms.
- Shift wrists to finish in a front support.

3 From a sit (or stand) on LB facing HB, grasp HB and. . .

a Long swing with 180° turn (may use double over-grip or mixed grip).

UNEVEN BARS

Between Bar Skills

b Long swing to a pullover on HB.

c Long swing to a single-leg overshoot (1-leg kip).

d Long hang kip.

UNEVEN BARS

Between Bar Skills

4 **From a stand or squat, stand on LB and grasp HB with double overgrip. Jump to...**

a Front support on HB.

b Immediate single leg cut to stride support on HB.

c Clear support position and execute a back hip circle on HB.

UNEVEN BARS

Between Bars Skills

5 Changing from HB to LB from a front support on HB facing LB.

a Lower slowly forward to grasp LB in overgrip and show a leaning handstand against HB.

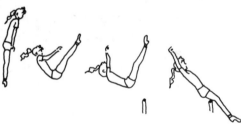

b Rotate backward while piking and bring both ankles near the HB. Extend the hips to arrive in a rear lying hang. Re-grasp LB to finish in a rear support position.

c Rotate backward while piking one leg to bring the ankle near the HB. Finish in a stride hang and re-grasp LB to show stride support.

UNEVEN BARS

Dismounts

1 Underswings

- From front support on LB facing either direction, cast to underswing dismounts. Including the following, a.) straddle. b.) stoop (pike). c.) straddle 180° turn. d.) one and a 180 half-turn, and e.) drop underswing.

- From a stand or squat stand on LB facing HB, grasp HB in overgrip and jump to underswing dismount.

- From a front support on HB facing out, cast to underswing dismounts.

- From a long hang in a pike-straddle position facing the LB with both feet on the LB, re-grasp one hand and then the other to overgrip position on the LB and execute a straddle sole circle dismount from the LB.

2 Dismounts from the LB From a front support facing out, cast to:

- Straddle on LB, jump off to landing.

- Squat on LB, jump off to landing.

- Flank dismount (both legs together to R or L).

- Straddle over LB to landing.

- Squat over LB to landing.

PARALLEL BARS

Support Series

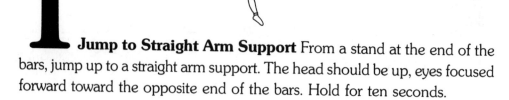

1 **Jump to Straight Arm Support** From a stand at the end of the bars, jump up to a straight arm support. The head should be up, eyes focused forward toward the opposite end of the bars. Hold for ten seconds.

Note: Preferred terminology would call this an "extended arm support." However, common usage is "straight arm support."

2 **Tuck Support** From a straight arm support, pull the legs upward to a tuck position with the knees slightly above the bars. Hold for ten seconds.

3 **One Leg "L" Support** From a straight arm support, raise the right leg to an "L" position, with the leg straight and slightly above bar height. Hold for five seconds and lower slowly to a support; repeat with the left leg.

PARALLEL BARS

Support Series

4
"L" Support From a straight arm support, raise both legs to an "L" position, both legs straight and slightly above bar height. Hold for five seconds.

5
Dips From a straight arm support, flex at the elbows, lowering the body below the level of the bars. Stop when the flex of the elbow reaches 90° Then extend the elbows and raise the body to a straight arm support. Repeat five times.

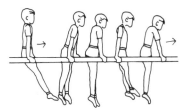

6
Support Walks, Forward and Backward From a straight arm support, shift body weight slightly from side to side while taking small hand steps forward with the hands. Walk three-fourths of the way across the bars, stop, and walk backward to the starting point.

PARALLEL BARS

Support Series

7 **Support Turn** From a straight arm support, shift the body weight to one side, release one arm, turn 90° and re-grasp, and change to a front support facing outward on one bar. Continue shifting the body weight, turn and change to a straight arm support to finish with a 180° turn. Practice the turn in the other direction.

8 **Support Hops** From a straight arm support, shrug the shoulders and quickly extend the arms downward to hop the hands forward slightly; continue hopping halfway across the bars, stop, and hop back to the starting position.

PARALLEL BARS

Support Swings

1 **Basic Swings (low)** From a straight arm support, raise the legs and hips forward and upward by pulling the upper chest into a slight body curve forward (hollow) position. Release this position and allow the body to swing freely backward, then forward. Maintain control and support for three complete swings.

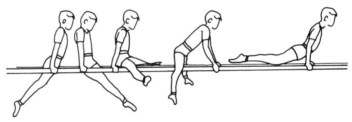

2 **Straddle Travels** From a low basic swing, straddle the legs at the peak of the forward swing finishing in a straddle support. Reach forward and lift the legs free of the bars; swing forward to another straddle support. After two to three travels, reverse the swing and return to the starting position.

3 **Straddle Travel Turn (corkscrew)** Swing both legs forward to a sitting position on the right rail. While turning to the left, raise the right leg up and over both bars. Finish in a straddle support facing the opposite direction of the starting position.

PARALLEL BARS

Support Swings

4 **Dip Swings Forward** At the peak of the backward swing, flex the arms slowly and swing forward. At the peak of the forward swing, extend the arms and swing backward. (Repeat three times.)

5 **Dip Swings Backward** Reverse the process in skill four above.

6 **Basic Swing, Front Dismount** On a backward swing, execute a dismount by pushing the legs and torso sideward, finishing in a cross stand.

I CAN DO GYMNASTICS

PARALLEL BARS

Support Swings

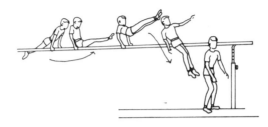

7 **Basic Swing, Rear Dismount** On a forward swing, execute a dismount by pushing the legs and torso sideward, finishing in a cross stand.

8 **Dip Swing Forward and Backward** Skills four and five are to be performed consecutively, without intermediate swings. (Repeat three times.)

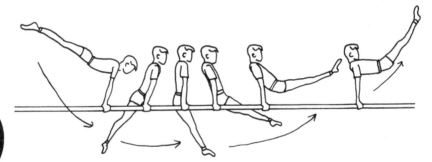

9 **Basic Swing (horizontal)** Slowly increase the height of the basic swing until the back reaches horizontal on both the front and back swings. At the peak of the swing the body should be in a slight body curve forward (hollow).

PARALLEL BARS

Upper-arm Support Swings
(bars should be set at head height).

1 **Jump to Upper-arm Support** From a mat or vaulting board, jump to an upper-arm support; elbows flexed 90°, shoulders held above the bars, and body straight (Hold for ten seconds.)

2 **Upper-arm Hang to "L" Hold** From an upper-arm support, raise the legs to an "L" position. (Hold for ten seconds.)

3 **Upper-arm Swing, (forward and backward)** From an upper-arm support, raise the legs and torso forward and upward to initiate a low basic upper-arm swing.

PARALLEL BARS

Upper-arm Support Swings

4 Back Uprise with Leg Support At the peak of a backward upper-arm swing, flex both legs to hook the feet on the bars. Push downward with the arms and legs to finish in a front leaning support.

5 Back Uprise (with spot) With the assistance of a spotter, perform several upper-arm swings. On the second or third backward swing, push down on the bars with the hands, moving the shoulders forward and upward over the hands. Extend the arms to a support position and swing forward.

6 Back Uprise to Support and Swing Forward Perform skill five without assistance.

PARALLEL BARS

Upper-arm Support Swings

7 **Front Uprise with Leg Support** At the peak of a forward upper-arm swing, pike slightly to hook the heels on the bars. Push downward with the hands and legs to finish in a rear leaning support.

8 **Front Uprise (with spot)** With the assistance of a spotter, perform several upper-arm swings. On the second or third forward swing, push down on the bars with the arms moving the shoulders forward and upward over the hands. Extend the arms to a support position and swing backward.

9 **Front Uprise to Support and Swing Backward** Perform skill eight without assistance.

PARALLEL BARS

Upper-arm Kips

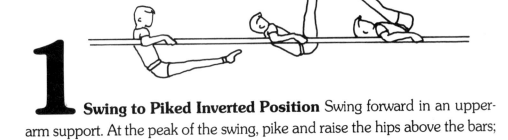

1 **Swing to Piked Inverted Position** Swing forward in an upper-arm support. At the peak of the swing, pike and raise the hips above the bars; hold this position with the legs parallel to the floor.

2 **Roll Forward to a Straddle Support** From an inverted piked position, roll forward while straddling the legs and extending the arms. Finish in a straddle support.

3 **Kip Forward to a Straddle Support** From an inverted piked support, extend the legs forcefully forward and upward extending the arms. Finish in a straddle support.

PARALLEL BARS

Upper-arm Kips

4 **Kip Forward to a Straddle Support (with spot)** From an inverted piked support, extend the legs forcefully forward and upward extending the arms. Finish in a straight arm support.

5 **Kip Forward to Support and Swing Backward** Perform skill four without assistance.

6 **Jump to Upper-arm Swing Forward and Kip to Support** From a mat or vaulting board, jump forward to an upper-arm swing forward with legs behind to a piked inverted support. Kip forward to support.

I CAN DO GYMNASTICS

PARALLEL BARS

Support Rolls and Shoulder Balances

1 **Straddle Sit, Tip-up to Straddle Shoulder Support, Return to Straddle Sit** From a straddle support, place the hands on the bars directly in front of the legs. Lean forward slowly placing the upper-arm on the bars in front of the hands. Shift the body weight onto the arms keeping the legs in contact with the bars. Return to a straddle support.

2 **Forward Straddle Roll** With the assistance of a spotter, roll forward through a tip-up, keeping the legs straddled. Continue to roll on the bars, sit up to finish in a straddle support.

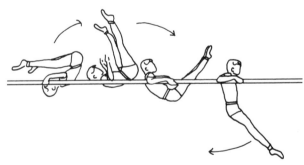

3 **Forward Roll to Upper-arm Swing** From a straddle sit, roll forward closing the legs together as the body becomes inverted. Extend the body forward and swing backward in an upper-arm support.

PARALLEL BARS

Support Rolls and Shoulder Balances

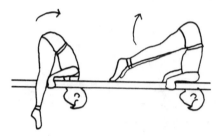

4 **Press to Straddle Shoulder Support (with toes on bars)** From a straddle sit, roll forward to a piked, straddled shoulder balance. Maintain contact with the bars with the toes/feet.

5 **Press to a Shoulder Balance (with spot)** From a straddle sit, slowly roll forward to a shoulder support and extend the hips while bringing the legs together. Hold the body in a vertical shoulder balance and slowly lower to a straddle sit.

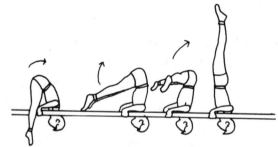

6 **Press to a Shoulder Balance and Hold** Perform skill five without assistance.

PARALLEL BARS

Support Rolls and Shoulder Balances

7 **Shoulder Balance, Forward Roll** Perform skill six, slowly pike and roll forward to a straddle support.

8 **Shoulder Balance, Roll Forward to Upper-arm Swing** Perform a shoulder balance, pike slightly, and roll forward. Rotate the arms to upper-arm support position and extend the body forward to swing backward in an upper-arm hang.

9 **"L" Hold, Press to Shoulder Balance** From an "L", raise the hips slowly while bending the arms to achieve a piked shoulder support. Straddle the legs and slowly extend at the hips to a shoulder balance position and hold.

PARALLEL BARS

Basket Swings
(bars should be set at head height)

1 **"L" Hang** From a rear lying hang, raise the legs to an "L" position and hold ten seconds.

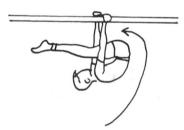

2 **"L" Hang Leg-lift** From an "L" hang, slowly raise the legs to bar level and lower back to an "L", repeat three times.

3 **Pull to Piked Inverted Hang** From a long hang with the feet resting on the mat, pull upward to finish in a piked inverted hang (basket).

PARALLEL BARS

Basket Swings

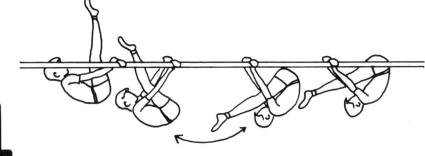

4 **Basket Swing** From a basket hang, rhythmically extend at the hips and alternately pull and push with the arms to generate a swinging motion.

5 **Jump to a Basket Swing** From a stand between the bars, jump upward pulling the legs to a pike position. Swing forward then backward in a basket position. (Spot for over-rotation.)

6 **"Jump-up" Kip to Support (bars lowered to chest height)** At the end of the bars, hang and place the feet at the base of the uprights. Flex and extend the knees several times simulating a swing. Then, push off with the feet and pull down on the bars with extended arms to achieve a support position.

PARALLEL BARS

Basket Swings

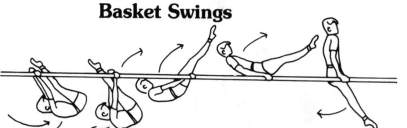

7 **Basket Swing to Kip (with spot)** Perform skill four. At the peak of the backward swing, quickly extend the legs upward and forward while simultaneously pulling down on the bars with extended arms. Finish in a straight arm support.

8 **Jump to Basket Swing and Kip to Support Swing (with spot)** Combine skills five and seven above, executing the kip without intermediate basket swings.

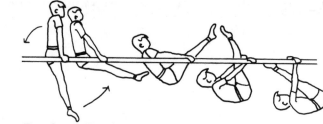

9 **Drop Back to Basket Swing (with spot)** From a straight arm support, push the hips back while lifting the feet upward and forward. Lean shoulders back and continue to rotate legs and hips to inverted position and basked swing forward and backward.

10 **Drop Kip to Support (with spot)** Perform skill nine, on the backward swing kip up to straight arm support.

PARALLEL BARS

Glide Kip

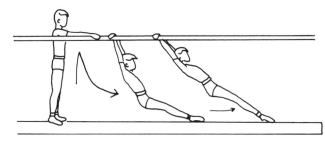

1 **Jump to Slide-glide** From a stand between the bars, jump lifting the hips backward and feet forward, keeping the feet in contact with the mat. (Wear socks so that the feet slide easily across the mat!)

2 **Glide, Touch Mat** Jump and glide out to touch feet on a stacked mat at the end of the glide swing. Then, hold a pike position on the backswing, keeping the feet just above the floor.

3 **Glide, Pike Back onto Mat** From a folded panel mat, perform skill two. On the backswing, pike and finish in the starting position.

PARALLEL BARS

Glide Kip

4 **Glide, Basket Swing** From a mat or vaulting board, jump and glide swing out to a stretched position. Then, lift the feet upward and backward while bending at the hips. Swing back in a basket position.

5 **Glide, Basket Swing, Kip to Support** Perform skill four, execute two to three basket swings and kip with straight arms to a support.

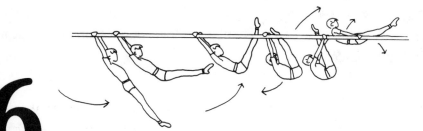

6 **Glide and Kip to Support** Perform skill five without intermediate basket swings.

STILL RINGS

Hangs and Holds
(rings lowered to head height)

1 **Grip and Hang** From a stand between the rings, grasp the bottom of the rings, palms facing inward and thumbs around. Slowly bend the knees and gradually take body weight finishing in a hanging position with the knees flexed and the feet lightly trailing the mat.

2 **Pull-up** From a kneeling position beneath the rings, grasp the rings and pull up to a flexed arm hang. Then, slowly lower to a straight arm hang.

3 **Flexed Arm Hang** Pull up to a flexed arm hang, hold, body extended with rings next to the shoulders. (Hold for five seconds.)

STILL RINGS

Hangs and Holds

- Tuck
- Pike (L Position)
- Straddle

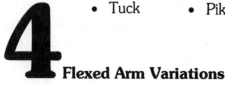

4 **Flexed Arm Variations**

5 **Tucked Inverted Hang** From a stand, lift the knees to a tuck position while simultaneously lowering the shoulders backward (straighten the arms). Maintain a tucked inverted position for five seconds and slowly lower to a bent knee hang.

6 **Piked Inverted Hang** Perform skill five with both legs extended.

STILL RINGS

Hangs and Holds

7 **Straight Inverted Hang** Perform skill six, while in the piked inverted hang extend at the hips. Keeping the body inverted, look at the mat beneath the rings, then return to a piked inverted hang and lower down.

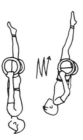

8 **Inverted Pull-up** From an inverted hang, lift the body up by flexing the arms. Pause momentarily when the hips are above the rings, then slowly lower down to an inverted hang. For additional balance, straddle the legs and place the feet on the ring straps. (Repeat three times.)

STILL RINGS

Rotations
(rings lowered to head height)

1 **Skin the Cat (dorsal hang)** From a piked inverted hang, rotate the torso and legs backward slowly while extending slightly at the hips. As the feet touch the mat, look at the mat, stand up, and release the rings.

2 **Skin the Cat (pull out)** Perform skill one, as the feet touch the mat, pull the hips upward, rotating the body forward. Finish in a piked inverted hang.

3 **Pull to Tucked Inverted Hang** From a hang, pull the knees up and rotate backward to a tucked inverted hang.

4 **Pull to Piked Inverted Hang** From a hang, pull the legs up to an L hang, rotate backward to a piked inverted hang.

STILL RINGS

Rotations

5 **Rotation Sequence** Flex arm hang; piked hang; piked inverted hang; skin the cat; skin the cat pull-out; extended inverted hang, flexed arm hang.

6 **Standing Dislocate** Stack two panel mat lengthwise below the rings. From a piked inverted hang, rotate backward and place both feet on the panel mats. Pull the rings sideward while rotating the hands out. Keep both arms straight and maintain pressure on the rings by pushing down. Extend at the hips and push the rings forward finishing in a stand on the mats.

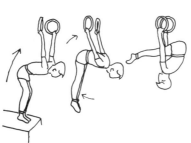

7 **Standing Inlocate** From a stand, flex forward to drop the chest below the rings, keeping the arms straight and extended forward. Pike at the hips and spread the rings sideward while rotating the hands outward. Continue to pike and finish in a piked inverted hang.

STILL RINGS

Swings
(rings six to twelve inches beyond extended reach)

1 **Jump to Hang (with spot)** From a stand, jump to the rings. Grasp the rings and hang for five seconds. Release the rings and land on the mat showing proper landing technique.

2 **Flexed Arm Hang, Release** Perform a flexed arm hang and hold for five seconds. Release the rings and land on the mat showing proper landing technique.

3 **Skin the Cat, Release** Perform a skin the cat. Look down at the mat and spot the landing target. Release the rings and land on the mat showing proper landing technique.

STILL RINGS

Swings

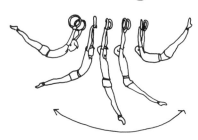

4 **Basic Swing** From a hang, raise the legs forward by "hollowing" the body into a forward curve. Release the forward curve and allow the torso and legs to swing the rings alternately backward on the forward swing and forward on the backward swing.

5 **Swing to a Piked Inverted Hang** Perform three basic swings as described in skill four. At the peak of the third forward swing, pike at the hips and rotate backward to a piked inverted hang.

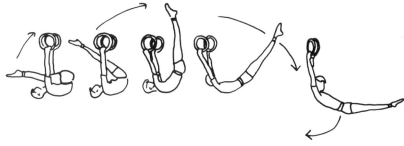

6 **Cast** From a piked inverted hang, simultaneously extend at the hips, direct the feet forward and upward, and flex the arms to pull the rings backward. Swing backward in a long swing.

STILL RINGS

Supports
(rings lowered to head height)

1 **Support** Stack two panel mat lengthwise below the rings. Grip the rings and slowly extend the arms, keep the feet in contact with the floor. Attempt to keep the rings parallel and next to the hips.

2 **Jump to Support** From a stand, grip the rings and slowly jump to a support position. Maintain the position as long as possible (up to 30 seconds).

3 **Support Lower to Hang** From a support, slowly flex the arms. As the feet touch the floor, flex the knees to maintain support on the hands. Lean backward slightly to allow the shoulder to pass below ring level. Continue lowering to a flexed knee hang.

STILL RINGS

Supports

4 **Support to Piked Inverted Hang** From a support, slowly bend the arms while piking at the hips. Rotate backward while lowering slowly to a piked inverted hang.

5 **One-leg Tuck Support** From a support, slowly bend one knee and pull the thigh up toward the chest. Hold for five seconds. Repeat with the opposite leg.

6 **One-leg "L" Support** Perform skill five with the legs extended . Hold the leg in the "L" position for five seconds.

STILL RINGS

Supports

7 **Dips** From a support, bend at the elbows and lower the body below the level of the bars. Stop when the bend of the elbow reaches 90°. Then extend the elbows and raise the body to a straight arm support. Repeat three times.

8 **Support Swing** From a support, slowly hollow the body to a forward body curve. Then allow the legs to swing back to a backward body curve. Swing several times, stop the swing, and finish in a straight arm support.

9 **Muscle-up to Support** Grip the rings with a "false grip" (wrist flexed over the top of the rings). Lower to a bent knee hang. Pull up to place both rings next to the chest. Slowly turn the rings out while rotating the chest forward to bring the shoulders above the rings. Extend the arms to finish in a straight arm support. If necessary, use the feet to push off the floor while rotating the rings.

STILL RINGS

Additional Skills

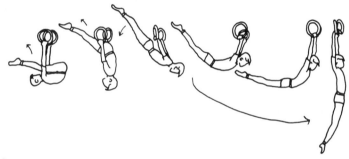

1 Inlocate Perform three basic swings. At the peak of the third backward swing, spread the rings sideward and rotate the hands inward. Pike at the hips and rotate forward to a piked inverted hang.

2 Dislocate From a piked inverted hang, extend at the hips directing the feet backward and upward. Simultaneously spread the rings and rotate the hands outward.

STILL RINGS

Additional Skills

3 **Back Uprise** Perform three basic swings. At the peak of the third backward swing, quickly pull down on the rings and hollow the body slightly Continue to keep pressure on the rings while moving the shoulders above the hands to a support position.

4 **Swing through Dismount** Perform three basic swings. At the peak of the third forward swing, bend the knees to a tuck position and rotate the body backward between the rings. Then release the rings and visually spot the landing target. Demonstrate proper landing technique, finish in a stand.

POMMEL HORSE

Support and Support Travels

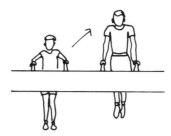

1 **Jump to a Support (pommels)** From a front stand, grasp both pommels and jump to a straight arm support.

2 **Jump to Support (end)** From a stand facing one end of the horse, place the hands on the end and jump to a front support.

3 **Jump through to Rear Support** From a front stand grasp both pommels, jump and tuck the legs through to a rear support.

> *What to practice:*
> - Keep arms straight in support.
> - Balance shoulders over the pommels.
> - Tuck through of the arms is smooth and continuous.

POMMEL HORSE

Support and Support Travels

4 **Simple Travel** From a front support on the pommels, shift the body weight to the right side. Change support by moving the left hand first to the right pommel, then the right hand to the end of the horse. Finish in a front support on the end of the horse. Repeat in the opposite direction.

5 **Simple Travel** From a front support on the end of the horse, execute two consecutive simple travels to the opposite end of the horse.

6 **Simple Travel Around the End** From a front support on the end of the horse, swing the legs around the end while changing to a cross support. Continue motion and move to a front support on the end of the horse, completing a 180° turn.

POMMEL HORSE

Leg Cuts and Leg Cut Travels

1 **1/2 Leg Cut Right and Left** From a front support on the pommels, swing the right leg up and over the right side of the horse. Maintain a straight arm support. Then, swing the legs back to a front support. Repeat using the left leg to the left side.

2 **Single Leg Cuts** From a front support on the pommels, swing the right leg sideward while shifting the body weight onto the left arm. Lift the right hand quickly and "cut" the right leg forward to a stride support. Then, reverse the process to finish in a front support on the pommels. Repeat using the left leg to the left side.

3 **Leg Cut Combination** Complete the following combinations: right leg over, left leg over, right leg back, left leg back, left leg over, right leg over, left leg back, right leg back.

What to practice:
- Shift weight side to side with leg cuts.
- Keep legs straight.
- Entire series should be smooth and continuous.

POMMEL HORSE

Leg Cuts and Leg Cuts Travels

4 Leg Cut Travel (downhill) From a front support on the pommels, execute a forward leg cut with the right leg. Swing the left leg over the horse while shifting the body weight to the left and move the right hand to the left pommel. Then, continue shifting the body weight to the left and move the left hand to the end of the horse. Swing the right leg back and execute a backward leg cut with the left leg to finish in a front support on the end of the horse.

5 Leg Cut Travel (uphill) Execute skill four, starting in a front support on the end of the horse and finishing in a front support on the pommels.

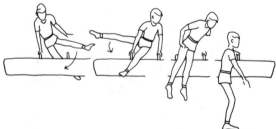

6 Leg Cut Dismount From a front support, execute two forward leg cuts. On the second cut, as the hand is lifted, pivot on the support arm 90° and push off the horse. Finish in a cross stand beside the horse.

POMMEL HORSE

Mounts and Vaults

Note: Skills one through four can be performed on a horse without pommels, a spotting box, or stacked mats.

1 **Flank Vault** From a front stand, place both hands on the body of the horse. Jump and swing both legs over the horse to the side and finish in a stand rearways. Repeat to the opposite side.

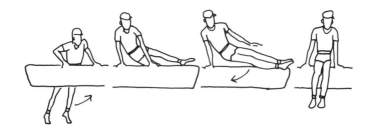

2 **Flank Vault to Rear Support** Perform skill one finishing in a rear support.

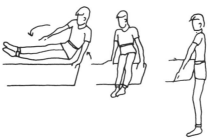

3 **Flank Vault Crossways** From a cross stand front, jump, and swing both legs over the horse to finish in a cross stand sideways.

POMMEL HORSE

Mounts and Vaults

Note: Skills five and six should be performed on a horse with pommels.

4 Flank Vault Crossways to Rear Support Perform skill three and finish in a rear seated support.

5 Flank Vault Sequences

A. From a front stand, place both hands on the pommels and execute a flank vault to rear support. Immediately execute a single leg cut backward in the direction of motion, then leg cut backward with the other leg finishing in a front support.

> *What to practice:*
> - Shift weight side to side.
> - Keep legs straight.
> - Entire series is smooth and continuous.

B. From a cross stand front, place both hands on the end of the horse. Jump and swing both legs over the horse, executing 1/4 turn to rear support on the end of the horse. Execute backward leg cuts as in "A" above.

POMMEL HORSE

Mounts and Vaults

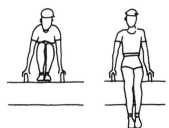

6 **Squat Through Sequence** From a front stand, place both hands on the pommels. Jump, tuck the legs, and swing through to rear support. Immediately execute a single leg cut backward, then leg cut backward with the other leg to finish in a front support.

POMMEL HORSE

Support Turns

1 Leg Cut Turn Out (Kehre) From a front support, cut the right leg forward, then cut the left leg forward and immediately pivot on the right arm to finish in a front support on the end of the horse. Repeat to the opposite side.

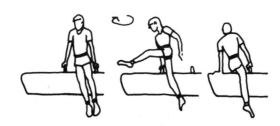

2 Single Leg Kehre Out From a front support, cut the right leg forward, then cut the left leg forward and immediately pivot on the right arm keeping the left leg above the level of the horse. Finish in a stride support on the end of the horse, left leg in front. Repeat to the opposite side.

POMMEL HORSE

Support Turns

3 **Leg Cut Turn In (Kehre)** Perform skill one starting in a front support in the downhill position.

> *What to practice:*
> * Strong arm push to shift weight.
> * Arms straight in support.
> * Finish with legs together.

4 **Single Leg Kehre In** Perform skill two starting in a front support in the downhill position.

POMMEL HORSE

Scissors and Circles

1 **Pendulum Swings** Swing the legs and torso sideward and upward in a continuous rhythmic movement from one side to the other:

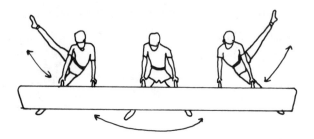

- Straddle Front Support.

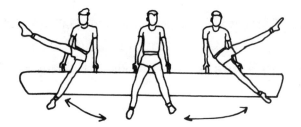

- Straddle Rear Support.

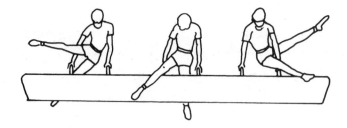

- Stride Support.

POMMEL HORSE

Scissors and Circles

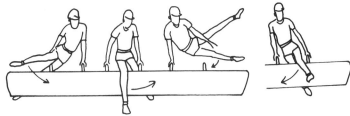

2 **False Scissor Forward** From a stride support right leg forward, execute three pendulum swings. On the third swing, cut the right backward over the left pommel, finishing in a front support pendulum swing with straddled legs. Repeat to the opposite side.

3 **Scissor Forward** From a front support, cut the right leg forward and pendulum swing to the left. Cut the right leg backward under the left as the left leg cuts forward. Finish in a stride support with the left leg forward. Repeat to the opposite side.

4 **Single Leg Circle** From a front support on the pommels, cut the right leg forward and continue the leg swing to cut the right leg backward over the left pommel. Repeat with the opposite leg.

POMMEL HORSE

Scissors and Circles

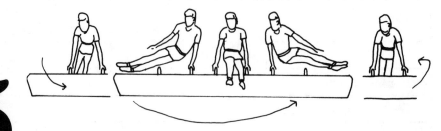

5 **Double Leg Pendulum Circle** From a front support, cut both legs to the left or right, then continue the motion and cut both legs to the opposite side. Perform the movement several times in succession.

6 **Circle in Cross Support (Loop)** From a cross stand front at the end of the horse, place both hands on the horse. Jump and swing both legs to the right, or left, and continue the circling motion to finish in a front support crossways at the end of the horse.

CHECKLIST FOR ADVANCED SUPPLEMENT

Skill	Date Skill Series Completed
FLOOR EXERCISES	
Back Limbers	
Back Walkovers Sequence	
Jump-Back to Stacked Mats or Skill Cushion	
Hand Stand Snapdowns	
Back Handsprings (FF)	
Skills into Back Handsprings	
Skill out of Round-off Back Handspring	
UNEVEN BARS	
Mounts	
Between Bar Skills	
Dismounts	
PARALLEL BARS	
Support Series	
Support Swings	
Upper-arm Support Swings	
Upper-arm Kips	
Support Rolls and Shoulder Balances	
Basket Swings	
Glide Kip	

Skill	Date Skill Series Completed
STILL RINGS	
Hangs and Holds	
Rotations	
Swings	
Supports	
Additional Skills	
POMMEL HORSE	
Support and Support Travels	
Leg Cuts and Leg Cut Travels	
Mounts and Vaults	
Support Turns	
Scissors and Circles	

I CAN DO GYMNASTICS

Glossary

BASIC BODY POSITIONS

Front Support: Any support position where your arms are extended and in front of your body.

Hollow: An extended body position with a slight contraction in the torso.

Inverted: Any position in which your lower body is moved into a position above your upper body. (When you stand on your hands, you are **inverted.**

Pike: Your body is flexed forward at the hips, while keeping the legs straight.

Prone: Lying face down with the body straight.

Rear Support: Any support position where your arms are straight and extended behind your body.

Squat: Support your body on the balls of the feet with the knees and hips flexed so that your seat is near, but not touching, your heels. Your torso is kept erect.

Straddle: A position in which your legs are straight and extended sideward.

Straight (Basic) Stand: Standing with your heels together, feet turned out (45°), legs straight, and torso and head erect with your arms down at your sides.

Straight or Stretched (Layout): In the layout position, your body is straight and completely extended.

Supine: Lying flat on your back with the body straight.

Support: Any position with the body above the apparatus where the weight is borne partially or completely by the arms.

Tuck: Your body is "curled up in a ball" when you are in the **tuck** position. The upper body is flexed forward, flexed at the hips, and the knees are flexed and pulled up to the chest.

JUMPS

Assemblé : Push upward off one foot, while swinging the other leg forward and upward, and bring your feet together upon landing.

Fouetté: Push off one leg while kicking the other leg forward and upward while executing a 180° turn, and land on your takeoff leg. Your other leg will remain extended rearward.

Hitchkick: Push upward off one leg while swinging the other leg forward and upward, switching legs in the air, and landing on the other foot, in a demi-plié .

Hop: Takeoff from one foot to land on the same foot.

Jump: Move from both feet to both feet.

Leap: Move from one foot to the other foot, showing flight.

Sissone: Step forward on one foot, bring the other foot forward to a position behind the first, jump and separate the legs to a split position, and land on the first leg.

Tourjeté : Push off one leg while kicking the other leg forward and upward executing a 180° turn, switch the legs in the air, and land on the first leg. Your takeoff leg ends extended rearward.

PREPARATORY MOVEMENTS

Chassé : Step forward with one leg and spring slightly off the floor. Extend the legs and close them together. Land on the back leg with the front leg raised in preparation for the next skill.

A chassé can be performed in a forward or sideward direction.

Demi-plié : This is the position of the legs and feet used in preparation for jumps, turns, and in landings. Your knees are slightly flexed and turned out along with the feet.

Hurdle: A long, low, and powerful skip step, which may be preceded by one or more running steps.

Lunge: A lunge is a position in which one leg is flexed approximately 90°, and your other leg is straight and extended. Your body is stretched and upright over the flexed leg.

HAND GRIPS

Overgrip: Grasping the bar with your thumbs pointing towards each other.

Undergrip: Grasping the bar with both of your thumbs facing out, away from each other.

Mixed grip: One hand in overgrip and the other in undergrip.

INVERTED SKILLS

Bridge: An arched position with your feet and hands flat on the floor and the abdomen up.

Cartwheel: The rhythm of the cartwheel is "hand, hand, foot, foot." Step forward with one foot, lift the other leg upward and backward while placing the hands onto the mat in front of the support leg. As the body becomes inverted, the legs remain in a straddled position (arms and legs look like the spokes of a wheel,) and lands one foot at a time.

Handstand: Hands are flat on the floor, shoulder width apart, and the body completely extended and straight, legs together.

Headstand: Place the hands and forehead on the floor in a triangular shape (head in front of hands), and extend the hips and legs straight upward over the triangular base of support.

Round-off: A round-off is a dynamic turning movement. Step forward and push off one leg while swinging the legs upward in a fast cartwheel type motion. As your body becomes inverted, execute a 90° turn, push off your hands, the legs are brought together just before landing. You should be facing the direction from which you started.

Tripod: Place the hands and forehead on the floor in a triangular shape (head in front of hands), and extend the hips above the triangular base. Your body is piked with the knees flexed, resting on your elbows.

GENERAL TERMINOLOGY

Arabesque: Basic standing on one foot. The free leg is rotated outward and held in the rear a minimum of a 45° angle to the support leg.

Body Wave: Executed from a contraction of the trunk, which is released by moving the body segments in succession to reach full extension.

Cast: From a front support (on uneven bars or horizontal bar) with your hands in overgrip. You will flex at the hips (90°) and immediately thrust the legs backward and upward while maintaining the support position with extended arms.

Clear: Movements in which only the hands (not the body) are in contact with the apparatus.

Dismount: A skill you perform from the apparatus to a controlled landing on a mat.

Flank: A skill in which your body passes over a piece of equipment with the side of your body facing the apparatus.

Flexibility: Flexibility is the range of motion through which a body part, such as the shoulders or legs, can move without feeling pain.

Panel Mats: Basic mats which are constructed of a single layer of resilient foam, ranging in thickness from one to two inches, that can be folded into panels approximately two feet wide.

Pivot: A sharp 1/2 turn around a single point of support, like one hand.

Rear: A descriptive term indicating that the body passes over or around an apparatus with the back of the body leading or facing the apparatus.

Rebound: A quick jump using very little flexion of the hips, knees, or ankles.

Sequence: Two or more positions or skills which are performed together creating a different skill or activity.

Spot: To spot is to physically guide and/or assist a gymnast while performing a skill. Coaches spot for safety and when they are teaching new skills.

Spotting also refers to focusing the eyes on a particular point or place while performing a skill, e.g. to "spot" a turn.

Snap: A very quick movement of the body, usually from a 3/4 handstand position, moving the feet to the ground bringing the body to a near upright position.

Stick: Slang: A gymnast "sticks" a landing when he/she executes a landing with correct technique and no movement of the feet.

Wedge: A developmental mat filled with soft, shock absorbent foam. Its distinct shape is a sloping triangle with various heights and widths.

One of the most confusing areas of gymnastics can be the descriptions of starting and finishing positions of the gymnast. The following illustrations should help to increase your understanding.

Front or Frontways   **Rear or Rearways**

Front or **Frontways:** the gymnast faces the apparatus, with the line of the shoulders parallel to the apparatus — Front stand.

Rear or **Rearways:** The gymnast has the back toward the apparatus with the line of the shoulders parallel to the apparatus — Rear stand.

Side, Cross, or Crossways

Side, Cross, Crossways: The gymnast has line of shoulders perpendicular to the apparatus. This is usually also indicated with Left or Right, Front or Back.

About the Author

USA **Gymnastics** is the national governing body for the sport of gymnastics in the United States for the United States Olympic Committee (USOC). The corporate body of USA Gymnastics is the United States Gymnastics Federation (USGF) which is recognized by the International Gymnastics Federation (FIG).

USA Gymnastics promotes the growth of gymnastics in the United States through a number of activities:

- Individual Professional Membership.
- Club, organization, and school membership programs.
- Gymnastics liability and medical programs.
- Gymnastics clinics, workshops and training camps for professionals and athletes.
- Educational resources development.
- Coaching accreditation.
- Safety certification.
- The USGF Junior Olympic competitive program that annually sanctions over 7,000 gymnastics competitions each year.
- Televised gymnastics events.
- International competitions, tours, and exhibitions.
- Gymnastics educational materials including magazines, periodicals, books, videotapes and public service information.
- Gymnastics related merchandise including apparel, novelties, and posters.
- A wide range of other activities.

For more information on USA Gymnastics, please contact:

USA GYMNASTICS
Pan American Plaza, Suite 300
201 S. Capitol
Indianapolis, IN 46225
(317) 237-5050.

MASTERS PRESS

A Division of Howard W. Sams & Co.

Fun With A Twist

I Can Do Gymnastics: Essential Skills for Beginning Gymnasts

United States Gymnastics Federation

Who can do gymnastics?

Anyone can!

I Can Do Gymnastics is the official student companion to the United States Gymnastics Federation's "Sequential II" program, the safest and most effective way to learn the basic gymnastics skills. With completely illustrated skill development series, progress charts, and information about each event, *I Can Do Gymnastics* is a must for every beginning gymnast.

> 144 pages * 7 X 10
> 0-940279-51-7 * $14.95
> b/w photos, charts, & drawings
> paper

Gymnastics: A Guide for Parents and Athletes

Rik Feeney

The most complete guide to the sport available, this unique volume takes the beginning parent and athlete through all the ups and downs of a gymnastics career. Including information on finding a club, injury prevention, the decision to compete, the decision to quit, and how to find a gymnastics scholarship to college, this book is sure to be the handbook for the next generation of gymnastics superstars. Approved by the United States Gymnastics Federation.

> 192 pages * 7 X 10
> 0-940279-43-6 * $14.95
> b/w photos, drawings, & cartoons
> paper

All Masters Press titles, including those in
the Spalding Sports Library, are available
in bookstores or by calling (800) 722-2677.